Annual Review of
BBC Broadcasting
Findings

Annual Review of
BBC Broadcasting Research
Findings

Number 9 1983

British Broadcasting Corporation

Enquiries about this Annual Review of Broadcasting
Research Findings should be made to

Broadcasting Research Department
BBC Broadcasting House
London W1A 1AA
Telephone: 01-580 4468, Extensions 8185 or 8732

Published by BBC Data, 1984
BBC Data Publications,
The Langham,
Portland Place,
London W1A 1AA.

ISBN 0 946358 16 8

Printed by
Letronic (Word Processing) Limited,
Esher, Surrey.

CONTENTS

Note on Definition of Social Grade/Class

Two methods of defining social grade/class, broadly similar but differing in detail, are used in this review. The definitions used by BBC Broadcasting Research up until the beginning of BARB joint BBC/ITV measurement (see Chapter I) were as follows:-

Class A: members of families in which the chief wage earner is a doctor, professor, member of the clergy, lawyer, architect; owner, director, senior executive of a large commercial or industrial organisation; senior civil servant; or high-ranking industrial technician such as scientist or consulting engineer (6% of the population).

Class B: members of families in which the chief wage earner is a bank clerk, more senior office worker, teacher, small employer, manager or shopkeeper of larger shops, supervisor in a factory, professional worker not coming into Class A (24% of the population).

Class Cx: members of families in which the chief wage earner is a skilled manual worker such as overseer, charge hand, bricklayer, carpenter etc., fitter, miner, electrician, junior clerical worker, shop assistant with responsibilities (40% of the population).

Class Cy: members of families in which the chief wage earner is a semi-skilled or unskilled worker. Apprentice, postman, caretaker, delivery man, labourer, shop assistant without responsibilities etc. (30% of the population).

The definitions used by BARB, and adopted for all BBC research, are shown below. The 'old' BBC definitions are also included for comparison.

Social grade (BARB)	Social status	Head of household's occupation	Approximately corresponding 'old' BBC grade
A	Upper middle class	Higher managerial, administrative or professional	A
B	Middle class	Intermediate managerial, administrative or professional	A
C1	Lower middle class	Supervisory or clerical, and junior managerial, administrative or professional	B
C2	Skilled working class	Skilled manual workers	Cx
D	Working class	Semi- and unskilled manual workers	Cy
E	Those at lowest levels of subsistence	State pensioners or widows (no other earner), casual or lowest-grade workers	-

The social grade of an informant is normally based on the occupation of the head of his/her household; if the head of household is retired, it is based on his/her former occupation. Where there is no such occupation, or information about it is unobtainable, social grade is assessed on environmental factors.

FOREWORD

The purpose of this Annual Review of the BBC's Broadcasting Research Findings is to make the results of a selection of some of our more significant or interesting research activities available to a wide public. We have in mind too fellow audience researchers in this and other countries, academic mass communications researchers, and - not least -the general public who through the Licence Fee fund the UK TV and radio services of the BBC.

As has been the tradition of these Reviews, a chapter (Chapter 1) has been devoted to up-dating the time series figures on the audiences to the TV Channels and Radio Services, both BBC and non-BBC, for the years 1981 and 1982. This includes an important methodological preface that summarises the changes and developments in the techniques used for measuring audiences. In the case of Television these took place under the joint BBC/ITCA BARB auspices beginning in August 1981. For radio there have been two phases of enhancement to the measurement system (the Daily Survey) introduced in May 1981 and April 1982 respectively.

This initial review of audiences in aggregate leads naturally into Chapter 2 in which the concept of an "audience" is discussed. There are a number of different definitions one can take for a programme's audience, beyond the one conventionally used in the standard routine reporting: that of the average over the duration of the programme in question. The concept, for example, of "Programme Reach" is an important one when considering the size of audience for a football match. By contrast, knowing how many people view a play from start to finish, the "Core Audience", is important when considering drama.

The remaining six contributions to this Review are drawn from the activities of the Department's Special Projects section.

Chapter 3 is concerned with the Falklands crisis. There was at the time some criticism of the BBC's coverage, both from Westminster and in the press. Some critics argued that undue prominence was given in BBC news coverage to the Argentinian viewpoint. To obtain independent evidence on the BBC news programmes as a source of information on the conflict and the public's views of the balance and objectivity of this coverage, a study was commissioned from an independent research organisation. The findings were reported within 72 hours of the decision being taken to sound public opinion on this important matter.

In late 1982 the forward planning was taking place and editorial decisions were being formulated for the launch of the BBC1 breakfast TV service "Breakfast Time". The department was actively involved in assisting the editorial team over this period. A summary of the public's appetite for breakfast television, and editorially what would be palatable at that time of day, is the subject of Chapter 4.

1982 also saw the ITAP Report and the Hunt Committee's Report on Cable. In parallel there were the experimental subscription TV services in which the BBC participated in a joint service operated with Visionhire in the London area ("Showcable"), and the BBC itself was formulating its plans for Direct Broadcasting by Satellite (DBS). Throughout this period of major activity, led by the Conservative Government with a particular interest in stimulating the domestic telecommunications industry, the department has been actively engaged in synthesising a wide range of data sources on the potential for cable and DBS in the United Kingdom (Chapter 5).

Chapter 6 concerns the views and radio listening behaviour of the population living in the editorial areas of Radio Highland and Radio Nan Eilean, in relation to these specific services. This study was conducted postally, the principal analysis variable being whether or not the respondent was or was not able to speak Gaelic.

The final chapters (Chapters 7 and 8) relate to two very different exercises in programme evaluation. The first concerned the effectiveness of a six part TV series on cigarette smoking in helping smokers who saw a programme in the series to give up. The second was a small-scale qualitative study of a TV series, QED, that set out to "do for general science, medicine and technology what "Wildlife on One" does for biology". It evaluated the performance of the first series, to assist in development and planning for the series to follow.

1. TRENDS IN VIEWING AND LISTENING: 1981-82

Peter Menneer, Head of Broadcasting Research Department

A Methodological Preface

It has been the practice of this Annual Review to publish each year the basic statistics on:

- the amount of viewing of and listening to each channel and service;

- hence their respective audience shares;

- and, additionally, the proportion of the population who view/listen at all to each channel/service on the average day: the concept of "daily patronage" or "daily reach".

The 1978/79 Annual Review, Number 6, contained 10 years' trend data reviewing the 1970's decade: 1970-1979. The following edition, Number 7, updated the figures to include the final year, 1980, before a number of methodological changes were introduced into the ways by which audiences are measured.

TV audience measurement under the auspices of the BBC/ITCA jointly owned research company, the Broadcasters' Audience Research Board, took effect from August 1981. The essence of this measurement system is a panel of c 3,000 UK representative private households in each of which a meter is attached to the TV set(s) and establishes when the set is on and to which channel it is tuned, and in addition a diary is kept for all household members aged 4 and over as to when they as individuals are viewing television.

In parallel the design of the BBC's Daily Survey, by which radio audiences are measured, was overhauled in two steps. The first took place in May 1981 when an entirely redesigned system of "recall aids" was introduced, to ensure that in each sampling point the interviewer is supplied with the previous day's complete programme schedules for all TV and radio services that are able to be received in that locality. In addition, from that date interviewers have been required to introduce themselves as from "Radio and Television Audience Research". The traditional BBC introduction had been demonstrated to lead to some respondents believing, understandably, that the study was more concerned about viewing of and listening to BBC broadcast services than to ITV and ILR.

The second phase of development took effect from April 1982 when the principal change was to move the place of interview from the street to the home. The purpose was in part to enable the Daily Survey interview to be used for placement of the BARB TV Audience Reaction Service booklet. But the object was also to improve upon our estimates of the audiences to radio, benefitting from the greater rigour in sample design that can be obtained from observing strict probability sampling principles down to the selection of individual streets within which the interviews have to be obtained, supplemented by quota controls to ensure the sample's representativeness in terms of sex, age and whether or not the person has a full-time job. The "trade-off" for this improvement in the quality of the sample was the need to halve the daily sample size: from 2,000 to 1,000 per day.

A fuller account of the survey methods currently employed for both television and radio audience measurement can be found in Pamela Reiss' contribution to the 8th edition of our Annual Review, Chapter 1 (1).

---

(1) Continuous Research for Television and Radio: the 1980's Approach.

It follows that for television we have two breaks in the continuity of time series data on audiences:

- in May 1981, with the redesigned Daily Survey documentation, and the introduction of the name "Radio and Television Audience Research" as the Department's data collection "subsidiary" on whose behalf the interviewer is working;

- and in August 1981 with the introduction of joint BBC/ITV audience measurement under BARB's auspices.

We equally have two points of discontinuity in the radio figures:

- in May 1981, as with television;

- and in April 1982, when the sample design was made more rigorous, and the interviews required to take place in respondents' homes.

For simplicity of exposition, in the tables to follow that relate to audiences to TV and radio over the years 1981 and 1982, we have deliberately shown no figures for the first two quarters of 1981. The May 1981 overhaul of the Daily Survey data collection design clearly led to some discontinuity in TV and radio figures. It is probably useful, therefore, to use the "n/a" (not available) convention to underline the clear break in time series.

There remains for radio, however, the technical problem of data linkage from Quarter 3 1981 to Quarter 2 1982 with the introduction of the more rigorous sample design. We are reasonably clear that the in-home interview situation, in particular, led to slightly higher levels of reported radio listening than hitherto. It is not possible to be absolutely precise about the extent of this effect, not least because April 1982 - as it so happened - coincided with the Falklands crisis and rather greater listening to radio over this period. Nonetheless, it is possible to apply approximate correction factors to the amounts of listening data for the 9 months ending March 1982. We have evidence of the design effect being slightly different between the four BBC network services on the one hand, and BBC Local and National Region radio services and commercial radio on the other. A correction factor of:

- x 1.15 for the 4 BBC National Networks

- x 1.20 for all other radio services

has therefore been applied to amounts of listening levels for these 9 months.

No equivalent adjustment has been applied to the Patronage (or Reach) figures. The discontinuity was less marked. The outcome of moving the interview into the home had relatively little effect on the number of people saying that they had listened the previous day at all to each service. What did change significantly was the number of programmes listened to, and hence the time spent, by those who tuned to each service at all on the average day. Nonetheless it should be noted that the patronage figures for the period Quarter 3 1981 to Quarter 1 1982 are slight underestimates - relative to the new Daily Survey norms established from April 1982.

Television

The average time spent per week viewing television by the average person aged 4 and over, across the United Kingdom, in 1982 was about $20\frac{3}{4}$ hours - or just under 3 hours per day. It should be noted that these figures do not include that element of TV viewing that takes place live through a VCR nor VCR time-shift viewing. By the close of 1982 it was estimated that about 15% of homes owned a VCR, and BARB has been taking steps to establish the number of hours of viewing of broadcast programmes that are as a result being missed. Clearly the understatement of audiences was rising throughout the year, as ownership of VCRs grew rapidly from a c 4% level in December 1981 to c 15% a mere 12 months later. It is likely that by the final quarter of 1982 the audience to broadcast TV programmes was under-stated by up to 5%, or 1 hour per head per week, through omission of the VCR audience.

Over and above the VCR phenomenon, there was some discussion in late 1982 about what appeared to be unusually depressed levels of viewing. One significant factor was the unusually warm weather for that time of year. The television audience (ie hours of viewing per head per week) is highly seasonal. Levels of viewing are much lower in the summer months. Indeed, the best predictor of the total television audience is an equation in which monthly mean daily temperature is taken as the sole independent variable:

$$H = 6.22 - 0.11T \qquad (R = 0.95)$$

where H = Average hours per day per home viewing television

T = Monthly mean daily temperature in $^{\circ}$C. (Source: BARB/AGB)

The final quarter of 1982 was on average 2°C warmer than the same months of 1981. One would expect this reason alone to account for a 5% lower aggregate level of viewing, year on year.

On 1 November 1982 S4C was launched, followed by Channel 4 1 day later on 2 November. The figures for their audiences relate to November and December and are included in the ITV 4th quarter aggregate.

Table 1: Average Amount of Viewing
Hrs: Mins per head of population per week (aged 4+)

	1981				1982				
	Q1	Q2	Q3*	Q4	Q1	Q2	Q3	Q4	Ave 82
BBC 1	n/a	n/a	7:21	10:12	9:24	7:49	6:15	8:11	7:55
BBC 2	n/a	n/a	2:05	2:55	2:59	2:48	2:10	2:15	2:33
All BBC	n/a	n/a	9:26	13:07	12:23	10:37	8:25	10:26	10:28
ITV	n/a	n/a	10:02	11:44	12:05	9:43	8:42	10:51	10:20
C4/S4C	n/a	n/a	-	-	-	-	-	(0.54)+	-
ALL TV	n/a	n/a	19:28	24:51	24:28	20:20	17:07	21:17	20:48

*August and September only

+November and December only

BARB/AGB

From the above estimates of amounts of viewing Channel Shares can be calculated. In 1982 the audience divided almost exactly between BBC and ITV (inclusive of Channel 4 and S4C in the final two months of the year). The BBC had a slight majority of the audience in the 2nd Quarter of the year, a major contributing element being coverage of Wimbledon in June - principally on BBC 2.

Over the first two months of Channel 4's and S4C's transmissions they obtained an average combined audience share of 4%. Their audiences are, as above, included in ITV's 4th Quarter aggregate.

Table 2: Channel Shares of Viewing
% of total viewing to each channel

	1981				1982				
	Q1	Q2	Q3*	Q4	Q1	Q2	Q3	Q4	Ave 82
BBC 1	n/a	n/a	37	42	38	38	36	38	37
BBC 2	n/a	n/a	11	11	12	14	13	11	13
Total BBC	n/a	n/a	48	53	50	52	49	49	50
ITV	n/a	n/a	52	47	50	48	51	51	50
C4/S4C	n/a	n/a	-	-	-	-	-	$(4)^+$	(4)
All TV	n/a	n/a	100	100	100	100	100	100	100

*August and September only

+November and December only

BARB/AGB

Another criterion of Channel "performance", not least for a broadcasting organisation that is funded by a licence fee, is the extent to which the public uses that service at all: the concept of Reach, or in traditional BBC terminology "patronage". To what extent does a Channel interest most people at least some of the time? The following two tables (Tables 3 and 4) show respectively Daily and Weekly Reach figures for each Channel.

It will be noted that over the course of the average week 86% of the population tunes at least once to either or both of BBC 1 and BBC 2. BBC 1's Weekly Reach is higher than that of ITV, despite an overall lower share of audience. BBC 2 is viewed daily by over a quarter of the population; and over the course of an average week by over two-thirds of people.

In the first two months of Channel 4 and S4C, their combined Daily Reach was just over 10%, rising to 40% over the course of a week.

Table 3: Average Daily Reach (Patronage) of Television
% of UK population (aged 4+)

| | 1981 | | | | 1982 | | | | |
	Q1	Q2	Q3*	Q4	Q1	Q2	Q3	Q4	Ave 82
BBC 1	n/a	n/a	51	63	63	53	45	53	54
BBC 2	n/a	n/a	22	32	34	28	23	26	28
Any BBC	n/a	n/a	56	69	69	60	51	59	60
ITV	n/a	n/a	56	63	59	51	45	56	53
C4/S4C	n/a	n/a	-	-	-	-	-	(12)+	-
Any TV	n/a	n/a	71	80	81	72	64	71	72

*August and September only

+November and December only

BARB/AGB

Table 4: Average Weekly Reach (Patronage) of Television
% of UK population (aged 4+)

| | 1981 | | | | 1982 | | | | |
	Q1	Q2	Q3*	Q4	Q1	Q2	Q3	Q4	Ave 82
BBC 1	n/a	n/a	81	89	88	84	78	85	84
BBC 2	n/a	n/a	62	75	77	68	62	68	69
Any BBC	n/a	n/a	83	90	90	86	81	87	86
ITV	n/a	n/a	82	88	81	77	72	82	78
C4/S4C	n/a	n/a	-	-	-	-	-	(40)+	-
Any TV	n/a	n/a	86	92	92	89	84	90	89

*August and September only

+November and December only

BARB/AGB

Programme makers are always interested in the composition of their audiences: in particular in terms of their sex, age distribution and socio-economic grouping. Eleanor Cowie's chapter in Annual Review Number 8 (2) showed a wide range of individual programmes and their widely varying audience compositions. It is also interesting, though, to observe the differing patterns of viewing to the Channels in aggregate - summing therefore across their schedules.

We have taken, in Tables 5-7, the first Quarter of 1982 as an example. This is, by definition, a span of three winter months with therefore relatively high levels of TV viewing.

We see the familiar pattern. Total viewing is lower amongst teenagers and reaches a peak amongst the retired population. The BBC has a dominant share of the viewing of children and adults in the age range 25-44. In terms of audience profiles within channel, nearly one-fifth of BBC 1 viewing is by children (aged 4-15).

Males view slightly fewer hours than females, with ITV's audience being the most female.

The Social Grade definitions, which are based on occupations, can be broadly defined as follows:

AB   Managerial and Professional

C1   Clerical

C2   Skilled working class

DE   Semi-skilled and unskilled working class and pensioners solely reliant on state pensions.

The number of hours spent viewing television rises sharply as social grade declines. The BBC has over 60% share of the AB audience, and less than half of the DE audience. It is still, however, the case that about two-thirds of the viewing to BBC 1 and BBC 2 is by the working class sector of the population and state pensioners (C2DE).

_____

(2) Viewing Patterns within the UK Population.

Table 5: Average Amount of Viewing – by Age, Sex, Class
Hrs: Mins per head of population per week (aged 4+)

		BBC 1	BBC 2	All BBC	ITV	All TV
AGE	4 – 7	8:14	1:54	10:08	6:40	16:48
	8 – 11	9:02	2:20	11:22	9:06	20:28
	12 – 15	7:25	2:15	9:40	8:01	17:41
All children		8:13	2:11	10:24	8:00	18:24
	16 – 24	6:09	1:59	8:08	8:35	16:43
	25 – 34	9:25	3:02	12:27	11:14	23:41
	35 – 44	8:56	3:00	11:56	10:19	22:15
	45 – 54	9:30	3:05	12:35	12:28	25:03
	55 – 64	10:13	3:34	13:47	14:25	28:12
	65+	11:03	3:40	14:43	16:22	31:05
All Adults		9:13	3:03	12:16	12:13	24:29
SEX	Male	8:48	2:49	11:37	10:36	22:13
	Female	9:15	2:56	12:11	12:09	24:20
SOCIAL GRADE	AB	8:52	2:43	11:35	7:02	18:37
	C1	9:06	2:45	11:51	9:28	21:19
	C2	8:45	2:46	11:31	11:56	23:27
	DE	9:32	3:17	12:49	14:36	27:25

BARB/AGB
Quarter 1, 1982

Table 6: Channel Shares of Viewing – by Sex, Age, Class
% of total viewing to each channel

		BBC 1	BBC 2	All BBC	ITV	All TV
AGE	4 - 7	49	11	60	40	100
	8 - 11	44	11	55	45	100
	12 - 15	42	13	55	45	100
All children		44	12	56	44	100
	16 - 24	37	12	49	51	100
	25 - 34	40	13	53	47	100
	35 - 44	40	14	54	46	100
	45 - 54	38	12	50	50	100
	55 - 64	36	13	49	51	100
	65+	35	12	47	53	100
All Adults		37	13	50	50	100
SEX	Male	39	13	52	48	100
	Female	38	12	50	50	100
SOCIAL GRADE	AB	47	15	62	38	100
	C1	42	13	55	45	100
	C2	37	12	49	51	100
	DE	35	12	47	53	100

BARB/AGB
Quarter 1, 1982

Table 7: Channel Profiles – By Age, Sex, Class
% of each Channel's viewing accounted for by ..... (sub-group)

		BBC-1	BBC-2	ITV	UK POPULATION
AGE	4 - 7	5	4	3	5
	8 - 11	7	6	6	7
	12 - 15	6	5	5	7
All Children		18	15	14	19
	16 - 24	9	9	10	14
	25 - 34	15	15	14	14
	35 - 44	14	14	13	14
	45 - 54	13	14	14	13
	55 - 64	12	13	14	11
	65+	19	20	21	15
All Adults		82	85	86	81
SEX	Male	47	48	45	49
	Female	53	52	55	51
SOCIAL GRADE	AB	14	13	9	15
	C1	21	20	17	19
	C2	37	36	40	35
	DE	28	31	34	31
TOTAL CHANNEL VIEWING/ POPULATION		100	100	100	100

BARB/AGB
Quarter 1, 1982

Radio

The average time spent listening to radio per week by the average person aged 4 and over was about $10\frac{1}{2}$ hours in 1982. This is just under half the time spent viewing television. Of these 10 hours of radio listening, Radio 1 accounts for nearly 3 hours, Radio 2 and ILR for about $2\frac{1}{2}$ hours each, Radio 4 for 1 hour and BBC Local Radio for about 45 minutes. It should, of course, be noted that these figures for BBC Local Radio and ILR are understatements of their audience in their own editorial areas. BBC Local Radio does not serve Scotland, Wales and Northern Ireland nor (in 1982) about 25% of England. Similarly ILR covers only about 75% of the United Kingdom. The amount of listening to these services in their respective editorial coverage areas is as follows:

Amount of Listening (per head per week) to BBC LR and ILR within their Editorial Areas

	(hours:mins)
BBC Local Radio	1:18
Independent Local Radio	3:20

Turning to the individual quarters, the Falklands factor stands out in Quarter 2 1982, when (relative to subsequent quarters - on a strictly comparable basis) unusually high levels of radio listening were observed - averaging close to $10\frac{1}{2}$ hours per head per week and falling gradually back in subsequent quarters.

The figures for the preceding three quarters have been adjusted as explained in the preamble, as far as possible to allow for methodological changes. What is particularly interesting and unusual (and is unaffected by these technical factors) is the rising levels in total radio listening from Quarter 3 1981 to Quarter 1 1982.

Table 8: Average Amount of Listening
Hrs: Mins per head of population per week (aged 4+)

| | 1981 | | | | 1982 | | | | |
	Q1	Q2	Q3*	Q4*	Q1*	Q2	Q3	Q4	Ave 82
Radio 1	n/a	n/a	3:03	3:05	3:05	2:57	2:59	2:54	2:58
Radio 2	n/a	n/a	2:23	2:35	2:35	2:24	2:18	2:22	2:25
Radio 3	n/a	n/a	0:20	0:12	0:10	0:07	0:12	0:10	0:10
Radio 4	n/a	n/a	1:06	1:09	1:17	1:08	1:05	1:07	1:09
Nat Regs etc	n/a	n/a	0:13	0:14	0:17	0:14	0:12	0:12	0:14
Local Radio	n/a	n/a	0:42	0:50	0:54	0:49	0:49	0:46	0:50
All BBC	n/a	n/a	7:47	8:05	8:18	7:39	7:35	7:31	7:46
ILR/Lux etc	n/a	n/a	2:20	2:32	2.49	2:45	2:36	2:19	2:37
All Radio	n/a	n/a	10:07	10:37	11:07	10:24	10:11	9:50	10:23

* Adjusted for changes in Daily Survey methods   BRD/Daily Survey

The service shares are, for the most part, unaffected by these technical issues. Radio 1 @ 29% had the largest share of total listening in 1982, followed by ILR @ 25%, Radio 2 @ 23% and Radio 4 @ 11%. Within their respective territories ILR and BBC Local Radio on average obtain:

Share of Listening to BBC LR and ILR
within their Editorial Areas

	%
BBC Local Radio	13
Independent Local Radio	33

ILR's share, while building over late 1981 into Quarter 1 1982, was clearly in decline from the Falklands quarter to the end of the year: from 27% down to 23%. The following BBC and ILR stations were opened during this two year span:

BBC Local Radio

Radio Jersey	15 Mar '82
Radio Guernsey	16 Mar '82
Radio Cambridgeshire	1 May '82
Radio Furness	25 May '82
Radio Northampton	16 Jun '82

Independent Local Radio

Northsound	27 Jul '81
Radio Aire	1 Sep '81
Centre Radio	7 Sep '81
Essex Radio	12 Sep '81
West Sound	16 Oct '81
Chiltern Radio	22 Oct '81
Radio West	27 Oct '81
Moray Firth Radio	23 Feb '82
Radio Wyvern	4 Oct '82
Red Rose Radio	5 Oct '82
Wiltshire Radio	12 Oct '82
Saxon Radio	6 Nov '82

Table 9: Service Shares of Listening
% of total listening to each service

			1981			1982			
	Q1	Q2	Q3*	Q4*	Q1*	Q2	Q3	Q4	Ave 82
Radio 1	n/a	n/a	30	29	27	29	29	30	29
Radio 2	n/a	n/a	24	24	23	23	23	24	23
Radio 3	n/a	n/a	3	2	2	1	2	2	2
Radio 4	n/a	n/a	11	11	12	11	11	11	11
Nat Regs etc	n/a	n/a	2	2	3	2	2	2	2
Local Radio	n/a	n/a	7	8	8	8	8	8	8
All BBC	n/a	n/a	77	76	75	74	75	77	75
ILR/Lux etc	n/a	n/a	23	24	25	26	25	23	25
All Radio	n/a	n/a	100	100	100	100	100	100	100

* Adjusted for changes in Daily Survey methods   BRD/Daily Survey

Within BBC Radio the term Daily "Patronage" has traditionally been used to define the number of people who listen at all on the average day to a particular radio service. This is synonymous to Daily "Reach". Figures for each service are shown in the following table. Note, as explained earlier, that relative to the figures from Quarter 2 1982 onwards the earlier figures are unadjusted for the methodological changes and will be slight underestimates.

On the average day just over half the population listens to radio at all, and just over 40% to a BBC radio service. Radio 1 has the highest daily Patronage @ 15%, Radio 2 and ILR @ 13-14%, Radio 4 @ 9%. It will be seen that few people listen to more than one station on any particular day: the sum of the Patronage figures is only slightly higher than the net 53%.

The use of Radio 4 was unusually high in Quarter 2 1982 which included the Falklands Crisis. As already noted from the share data, ILR's figures were rising over the nine months leading to early 1982 and then began to fall back later in the same year.

Table 10: Average Daily Patronage (Reach) of Radio
% of UK population (aged 4+)

	1981				1982				
	Q1	Q2	Q3*	Q4*	Q1*	Q2	Q3	Q4	Ave 82
Radio 1	n/a	n/a	14	15	15	16	15	15	15
Radio 2	n/a	n/a	12	13	13	14	13	13	13
Radio 3	n/a	n/a	2	1	1	1	1	1	1
Radio 4	n/a	n/a	9	9	9	10	9	9	9
Nat Regs etc	n/a	n/a	2	2	2	2	2	2	2
Local Radio	n/a	n/a	4	4	5	5	5	5	5
All BBC	n/a	n/a	38	40	40	44	41	41	41
ILR	n/a	n/a	11	12	13	15	14	13	14
Lux etc	n/a	n/a	1	+	+	+	+	+	+
Any Radio	n/a	n/a	47	49	51	56	52	51	53

*Not adjusted for changes in Daily Survey methods.   BRD/Daily Survey

+ Less than 0.5%

Weekly Patronage figures for the individual services cannot be derived from the Daily Survey, since it involves different samples of the population being interviewed each day about their previous day's listening.   However, it is interesting to note the Weekly Patronage figures yielded by the following question asked at the close of the Daily Survey interview - albeit relating to a population aged 12 and over:

"Have you listened to ..... (service) in the last seven days?"

	Weekly Patronage Population aged 12+
	%
Radio 1	40
Radio 2	34
Radio 3	6
Radio 4	21
Nat Regs etc	10
Local Radio	19
Any BBC	78
ILR	39
Any Radio	89

BRD/Daily Survey
9 - 22 May 1983

About 9 in 10 of the population aged 12 and over listen to radio at least once over the course of the average week, and over three-quarters listen to a BBC service. 4 in 10 listen at least once a week to Radio 1 (ILR's figure being effectively identical), 1 in 3 to Radio 2, and 1 in 5 to Radio 4 and BBC Local Radio. Radio 3 is clearly used more selectively than the other networks, achieving a high Weekly Patronage of 6% (relative to its Daily Patronage).

Tables 11 - 13 show the structure of each service's audience in terms of sex, age and class composition. It will be seen that they differ dramatically - the radio audience being highly segmented in that sense.

Total radio listening in aggregate is highest amongst 16-24's and then slowly but systematically declines with increasing age. There is more listening to radio among women than among men. In terms of the socio-economic groupings, it is the middle classes who do the most radio listening.

Taking now the services in turn:

Radio 1

Not surprisingly the highest figures for Radio 1 occur amongst the 16-24's. Children (aged 4-15) account for 12% of Radio 1's listening, and the age spread 16-34 for a further two-thirds. Turning the figures around, we also see that, for people up to the age of 24, Radio 1 is their dominant radio fare at c 60%, with ILR and Luxembourg accounting for 25%.

The social grade group who do the most Radio 1 listening are people from skilled working class families (C2). c 10% of Radio 1's audience is from the middle class (AB).

Radio 2

Radio 2 is the dominant service for all age groups from 35 upwards, and it accounts for about a third (or more) of all radio listening of people aged 45 and above. Nearly two-thirds of Radio 2's audience is aged 45 and over.

There is a slight female bias in Radio 2's listening.

Radio 3

Radio 3's listening rises with both age and class. Alone of the radio networks, it is listened to more by men than by women.

Radio 4

Like Radio 3, Radio 4 listening rises with both age and class - though the middle classes (AB) account for slightly less of Radio 4's audience (@ 33%) than of Radio 3's audience (@ over 40%). A half of Radio 4's listening is by people aged 55 and above.

Radio 4 is the network with the most marked female profile: nearly two-thirds of Radio 4 listening is by women.

BBC National Regions

The composite audience to BBC's radio services in Scotland, Wales and Northern Ireland is the most middle-aged and above of all radio services. Only about a quarter of their combined audience is under the age of 45.

BBC Local Radio

The combined audience for the BBC (English) Local Radio stations is similar in their characteristics to those of the National Region services: a mature age structure. Local Radio is relatively little tuned to by the middle classes (AB).

ILR

In age terms ILR, as one would expect, lies between Radio 1 and Radio 2. Its class structure, however, is similar to BBC Local Radio: the working class groups (C2DE) account for three-quarters of ILR's audience - in aggregate.

Table 11: Average Amount of Listening – by Age, Sex, Class
Hrs: Mins per head of population per week (aged 4+)

		R1	R2	R3	R4	Nat Regs etc	BBC LR	All BBC	ILR/ Lux etc	All Radio
AGE	4 – 15	2:01	0:17	–	0:04	0:01	0:06	2:29	0:49	3:18
	16 – 24	8:31	0:45	0:04	0:14	0:02	0:13	9:49	3:18	13:07
	25 – 34	5:30	1:39	0:06	1:01	0:05	0:24	8:45	3:29	12:14
	35 – 44	2:54	3:11	0:11	1:23	0:09	0:46	8:34	2:53	11:27
	45 – 54	1:17	3:53	0:13	1:33	0:16	1:04	8:16	2:32	10:48
	55 – 64	0:31	3:56	0:17	1:53	0:22	1:41	8:40	2:03	10:43
	65+	0:17	2:58	0:16	2:20	0:25	1:41	7:57	1:26	9:23
All Adults		3:09	2:43	0:11	1:25	0:13	0:58	8:39	2:37	11:16
SEX	Male	2:54	2:06	0:11	0:54	0:10	0:47	7:02	2:10	9:12
	Female	3:00	2:29	0:08	1:27	0:12	0:51	8:07	2:27	10:34
SOCIAL GRADE	AB	1:55	2:20	0:28	3:02	0:16	0:26	8:27	1:31	9:58
	C1	2:46	2:41	0:14	1:40	0:11	0:45	8:17	2:10	10:27
	C2	3:45	2:11	0:04	0:41	0:09	0:46	7:36	2:32	10:08
	DE	2:44	2:09	0:04	0:40	0:11	1:02	6:50	2:30	9:20

BRD/Daily Survey
Quarter 1, 1983

Table 12: Service Shares of Listening – By Age, Sex, Class
% of total listening to each service

		R1	R2	R3	R4	Nat Regs etc	BBC LR	All BBC	ILR/ Lux etc	All Radio
AGE	4 – 15	59	9	*	3	1	3	75	25	100
	16 – 24	64	6	1	2	*	2	75	25	100
	25 – 34	46	13	1	8	1	3	72	28	100
	35 – 44	25	28	2	12	1	7	75	25	100
	45 – 54	12	37	2	14	2	10	77	23	100
	55 – 64	5	36	3	18	3	16	81	19	100
	65+	3	32	3	25	4	18	85	15	100
All Adults		27	24	2	13	2	9	77	23	100
SEX	Male	31	23	2	10	1	9	76	24	100
	Female	28	24	1	14	2	8	77	23	100
SOCIAL GRADE	AB	19	24	5	30	3	4	85	15	100
	C1	26	26	2	16	2	7	79	21	100
	C2	36	22	1	7	1	8	75	25	100
	DE	29	23	1	7	2	11	73	27	100

* Less than 0.5%

BRD/Daily Survey
Quarter 1, 1983

Table 13: Service Profiles – By Age, Sex, Class
% of each service's listening accounted for by .... (sub-group)

		R1	R2	R3	R4	Nat Regs etc	BBC LR	All BBC	ILR Lux etc	All Radio	Popul ation
AGE	4 - 7	2	-	-	-	-	-	1	1	1	5
	8 - 11	3	1	-	-	1	1	1	2	2	7
	12 - 15	7	1	1	1	1	1	4	4	4	7
All Children		12	2	1	1	2	2	6	7	7	19
	16 - 24	35	4	4	3	3	3	16	15	16	14
	25 - 34	30	11	10	14	7	8	19	23	19	15
	35 - 44	14	19	16	17	12	14	16	19	17	12
	45 - 54	5	22	17	16	18	17	14	15	14	12
	55 - 64	2	22	24	20	25	25	14	12	13	12
	65+	2	20	28	29	33	31	15	9	14	16
All Adults		88	98	99	99	98	98	94	93	93	81
SEX	Male	48	45	55	37	43	46	45	45	45	49
	Female	52	55	45	63	57	54	55	55	55	51
SOCIAL GRADE	AB	9	13	43	33	16	7	15	8	13	17
	C1	20	24	30	29	21	19	23	18	22	22
	C2	39	29	13	18	23	29	31	35	32	32
	DE	32	34	14	20	40	45	31	39	33	29
TOTAL SERVICE LISTENING/ POPULATION		100	100	100	100	100	100	100	100	100	100

BRD/Daily Survey
Quarter 1, 1983

2. THE TELEVISION AUDIENCE

Pamela Reiss, Manager, Output (Continuous Services)

How many people watched Programme A?

A simple question, but the answer relies on two definitions: what is viewing and what is an audience?

This paper sets out to define these concepts in terms of the BARB measurement system which has been in operation since August 1981 (1). Four different definitions of audience size are proposed and the final section of the paper exemplifies the relationships between three of these concepts for feature films.

Viewing

In the theatre or cinema, the audience is captive. Allowing for a few late-comers and people who leave before the end of a performance, the size of the audience remains constant. Television audiences, however, are not static. In any one household, Mr. Smith may begin watching a programme - ten minutes later, Mrs. Smith joins him - five minutes later, Mr. Smith goes to the pub - Junior Smith comes in the room and wants to watch a different programme. Magnify this and similar situations over the population, and the concept of viewing becomes extremely difficult to define for measurement of programme audiences.

Under the BBC's Daily Survey the problem was resolved by defining a viewer as someone who watched more than half a programme or part-progamme if it was longer than an hour. Thus one was either a viewer or not. This definition was extremely crude and relied on the informant remembering not only what he had watched on which channel, but also how much of it he had seen.

Under BARB, we have moved one step nearer to monitoring viewing situations. The meter on the TV set monitors minute-by-minute adjustments, recording when the set is switched on and to which channel it is tuned. Data on individuals is collected by a simple diary in which each household member, plus any guests, records his or her presence in the TV room for at least 8 minutes in a clock quarter-hour. The two sets of data are married together to yield audience estimates (1). Thus, although the BARB system provides highly accurate and sensitive set data, the information on individuals still relies on people filling in their diaries correctly and is only sensitive to clock quarter-hours. It is to be hoped that the system to be adopted in 1984 will improve the sensitivity and accuracy of the data on individuals.

Nevertheless, BARB and 'son-of-BARB' mean that a measurement system exists to monitor viewing throughout a programme's transmission time. We are still left with the problem of defining an audience.

Audience Size

Take, for example, Top of the Pops. It could be argued that a viewer is someone who has seen at least 5 minutes of the programme to find out, say, what is Number One in the Charts. At the other extreme, the audience to The Man Alive Debate could be defined as those people who watched all of the programme in order to hear the reasoned arguments on both sides. The audience to a football match, however, say the F.A. Cup Final, could be defined as those people who saw any of the match.

These situations give rise to two basic definitions of an audience:

    The Core Audience - the number of people who saw all of the programme.

---

(1)   For more detail, see the Annual Review of BBC Broadcasting Research Findings No. 8 1981/2.

The Total Reach - the number of people who saw any of the programme.
('Any' itself can be defined in terms of at least 5 minutes, more than half, etc.)

The audience estimates published weekly by BARB adhere to neither of these definitions! They are a compromise, aimed at providing a common currency of measurement for all programmes.

BARB's definition of a programme audience is the number of people who watched the programme averaged over its transmission time - an AVERAGE AUDIENCE. Given the differing nature of programmes and their varying lengths, if one is wishing to compare the sizes of audiences for all programmes, this is the <u>only definition which makes sense.</u> It takes account of all the complex viewing situations exemplified at the beginning of this paper.

Finally, there is the PEAK AUDIENCE, i.e. the maximum number of people watching at any time during the programme.

Take Sportsnight on BBC-1 for example. On one particular Wednesday, it ran from 10.00 pm to 11.15 pm, during which time many people were going to bed. It opened with an audience of 7 million which steadily declined to a figure of 2½ million at the close. The following chart identifies the four different audiences which one could choose to apply to that edition of Sportsnight.

Table 1   **Sportsnight: BBC 1 Wed (10.00 - 11.15 pm)**

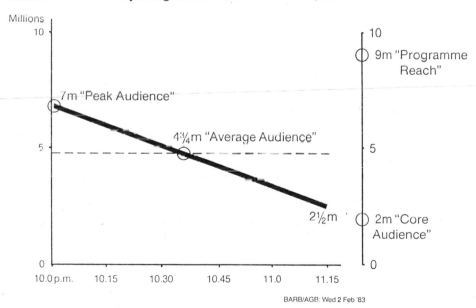

BARB/AGB: Wed 2 Feb '83

- Its Average Audience was $4\frac{3}{4}$ million.

- Its Peak Audience, when it opened, was 7 million.

- The number of people who saw Sportsnight at all, its Total Reach, was 9 million.

- The number of people who watched from beginning to end, the Core Audience, was 2 million.

To Summarise

There are basically four definitions of audience:

Average Audience - The number of people who watched the programme averaged over its transmission time - the BARB programme estimates.

Core Audience - The number of people who saw all of the programme.

Total Reach - The number of people who watched some part of the programme.

Peak Audience - The maximum number of people watching at some time during the programme.

The average audience estimates which appear in the BARB Weekly Report should be taken as best estimates for comparative purposes.

For certain types of output, notably long programmes such as sporting events, feature films, variety gala performances etc., the total reach gives a more meaningful description of the number of viewers. It is also a useful concept to employ for series and serials, e.g. the reach of, say, Smiley's People, is the number of people who saw at least one episode.

In other particular instances where the balance achieved by the whole programme is most important, it is the core audience which perhaps represents the most meaningful definition of audience.

By way of example, the following table shows the average audience, the total reach and the core audience for each televised World Cup match in 1982.

Table 2   **World Cup Grandstand (BBC-1) and World Cup '82 (ITV)**

(All figures rounded to nearest ½ million)

MATCH		CHANNEL	DATE	TIME	AVERAGE AUDIENCE (ie BARB audience estimates) millions	TOTAL REACH (No. who saw any of match) millions	CORE AUDIENCE (No. who saw all of match) millions
Brazil	v USSR	BBC-1	June 14	19.35	7½	12½	2½
Italy	v Poland	ITV	June 14	15.50	5½	10½	1
Scotland	v New Zealand	ITV	June 15	19.45	11½	16½	4½
England	v France	BBC-1	June 16	16.15	9	15½	2½
Spain	v Honduras	ITV	June 16	19.35	9	14½	3
N.Ireland	v Yugoslavia	ITV	June 17	19.45	11	16½	3½
Brazil	v Scotland	BBC-1	June 18	19.35	11½	18	4
Italy	v Peru	ITV	June 18	15.50	6½	12½	1½
Poland	v Cameroon	ITV	June 19	16.05	6½	10	2
England	v Czechoslovakia	ITV	June 20	15.45	10½	13	2½
N.Ireland	v Honduras	ITV	June 21	19.35	11½	18	4
Scotland	v USSR	BBC-1	June 22	19.45	11	17½	4
Peru	v Poland	ITV	June 22	15.45	6	12½	1½
Brazil	v New Zealand	ITV	June 23	19.35	9½	15½	3
Yugoslavia	v Honduras	ITV	June 24	19.35	9	14	3
Spain	v N.Ireland	BBC-1	June 25	19.35	9	15½	2
England	v Kuwait	ITV	June 25	16.00	9	14	3
Austria	v France	BBC-1	June 28	16.15	5½	12	1½
Poland	v Belgium	ITV	June 28	19.45	8½	14	2½
England	v Germany	BBC-1	June 29	19.15	11½	17½	2½
Argentina	v Italy	ITV	June 29	15.50	7	12½	1½
N.Ireland	v Austria	BBC-1	July 1	16.15	7	13	2
Belgium	v Russia	ITV	July 1	19.45	8½	14½	2½
W.Germany	v Spain	BBC-1	July 2	19.00	8	15	1
Brazil	v Argentina	ITV	July 2	16.00	7	12½	2
Poland	v Russia	BBC-1	July 4	19.50	6½	12	1½
N.Ireland	v France	ITV	July 4	15.50	5½	9	1½
Italy	v Brazil	BBC-1	July 5	16.05	7	13½	2
England	v Spain	ITV	July 5	19.35	14	19	4
Italy	v Poland	BBC-1	July 8	16.05	5½	11	1½
W.Germany	v France	ITV	July 8	19.35	10½	18½*	2
Final (Italy v W.Germany)		BBC-1	July 11	18.30	7	11½	2
Final (Italy v W.Germany)		ITV	July 11	18.15	6½	11½	2

FINAL (over both channels)   6½   19½

---

* NB extra time played.

Feature Films: Average Audience, Reach And Core

In order to investigate the relationships between these three measures of audience size for feature films, data was analysed for about 200 films broadcast by BBC-1, BBC-2 and ITV in the Autumn of 1982.

Reach and Average Audience

As Chart 1 indicates, there is a strong positive correlation between reach and average audience for feature films.

The high correlation (0.99) between the two sets of figures implies that the equation of the straight line which best fits the data can be used with reasonable accuracy to predict the reach of a film from the BARB average audience figure.

The equation of this line is:

Reach = 0.83 + (1.26 x Average Audience)

Thus, if a film has an average audience of say 8 million, its reach is likely to be:

0.83 + (1.26 x 8), i.e. 11 million

As might be expected, however, there were far fewer films with average audiences of 10 million and above (less than 10% of the total sample). The relationship between average audience and reach for these films (i.e. the major blockbusters such as Star Wars) is less well defined. It would appear that, above a certain level, the higher the average audience the smaller the increment to the total reach of the film (2).

Core Audience v Average Audience

Chart 2 indicates that there is also a fairly strong correlation between the core and average audience for feature films.

The equation of the straight line which best fits all the data is:

Core Audience = (0.55 x Average Audience) - 0.12

Thus, as a rough indication, the core audience of a film is likely to be just over half of the average audience.

It was found, however, that the relationship changed as the average audience increased. The slope is steeper as the audience size increases, i.e. the core audience comes closer to equalling the average audience as the audience size increases. The data was therefore split, obtaining three different equations for predicting the core audience depending upon the size of the average audience.

---

(2) This may well be the result of extensive publicity for certain films throughout the media, creating increased awareness among viewers and thus a greater likelihood of a larger number of people watching the film and seeing all of it.

Chart 1: **Reach vs Average Audience to Feature Films**

Correlation Coefficient = 0.99

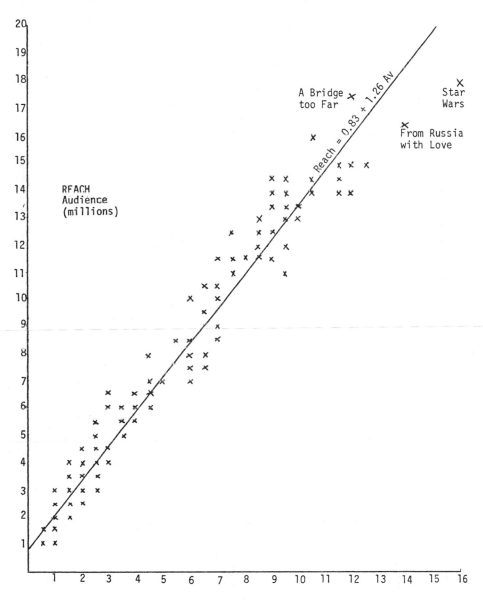

BARB Average Audience (millions)

Chart 2:

Core Audience vs Average Audience for Feature Films

Correlation Coefficient = 0.95

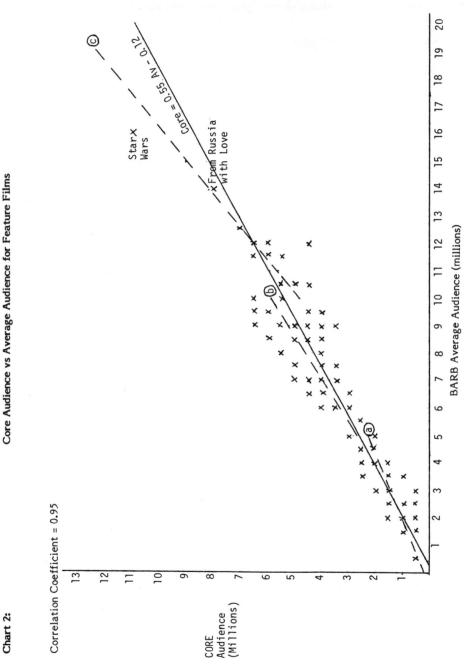

BARB Average Audience (millions)

CORE Audience (Millions)

-    When the average audience is below 5 million
     core = (0.43 x Average Audience) + 0.11

-    When the average audience is between 5 and 10 million
     core = (0.60 x Average Audience) - 0.29

-    When the average audience is greater than 10 million
     core = (0.84 x Average Audience) - 3.62

Reach v Core Audience

There was also found to be some degree of correlation between the figures for the reach and the core audiences to films. As would be expected, the length of the film has an effect on these figures, that is, the longer films tended to have fewer people watching all of the film (core audience) and more watching at least some of it (reach). Some exceptions to this were particularly well known, popular, or recently publicised films such as 'The Dambusters' and 'Star Wars'.

In conclusion, therefore, the data provides evidence of definite relationships between the average audience, the core audience and the reach of feature films. The core audience and reach figures can therefore be predicted with some degree of confidence using the above equations. The only real exceptions are the films with above average audiences - major films where there may be far less difference than expected between the core, average audience and reach figures.

3. THE FALKLANDS
AND THE BBC

Pam Mills, Head of Special Projects

Introduction

On 2nd April 1983, Argentinian forces invaded the Falklands. From that date until after the end of hostilities, on 14th June, the Falklands dominated the media. Large audiences were reported for specific TV news broadcasts, and the general impression was given that the British public was glued to their television screens for the latest news, in much the same way as they are reputed to have gathered around their radio sets in the Second World War.

The first part of this paper is concerned with the extent to which this popular impression is based on reality - that is, whether news audiences were, in fact, higher from April to June 1983 than they otherwise would have been; whether people were more likely to tune in to TV news on a particular night or over a week; and whether people saw more news bulletins.

In times of crisis, so it is said, the British public turns to the BBC as the source of authoritative, definitive information about events. In the early days of the Falklands crisis, the BBC was criticised in the press and in Parliament for unpatriotic reporting in failing to identify strongly enough with the British troops. The second part of this paper addresses itself to these issues - the extent to which viewers chose BBC rather than ITV as their source of news about the Falklands; and what the general public thought about the balance of TV's coverage.

Two main data sources have been used. First, information about what people did - when and how much TV they watched - is derived from BARB Audience Measurement Service (1). Meters on sets in a representative sample of around 3,000 UK homes register when the set is on and to which channel it is tuned; diaries, completed by each individual in these households, provide information on who is viewing. Second, the public's opinions of and attitudes to TV coverage were collected in two surveys conducted during the conflict in mid-May and after it finished in late June.

Summary

1. Over the whole period of the Falklands conflict, audiences to news programmes were generally higher than they otherwise would have been.

2. Some individual BBC and ITV news bulletins had very high audiences indeed (up to 17.25 million) and others showed increases or, at least, a smaller decrease in audience size than would have been expected for seasonal reasons.

3. In spite of this, only around half the population (aged 4+) saw at least one of the five main news bulletins on an average weekday, and although the number was slightly higher in the early days of the conflict than just before it, it had fallen back by June.

---

(1)   For full details of the BARB technique, see Pamela Reiss: Continuous Research for Television and Radio: The Eighties Approach; Annual Review BBC Broadcasting Research Findings No. 8 1981/2.

4.   Any changes in behaviour were, moreover, fairly small, with a slightly increased tendency to view at all and a marginal increase in the frequency of viewing.

5.   The public turned to BBC's news more than to ITV's during the conflict. This was reflected both in their behaviour and in the view that, on balance, the BBC had given the best coverage of the crisis.

6.   Overall, the BBC had a high degree of public support; over eight in ten said the BBC had behaved in a responsible manner in its coverage of the Falklands Crisis.

7.   But there was, in the early days, criticism from a significant minority of the balance of information between the British and Argentinian points of view; one in three felt the BBC was giving too much information from the Argentinian point of view; 30% thought they were not giving enough information about the British point of view. Though the level of criticism had declined by the end of the conflict, it remained at over one in five.

8.   The conflict raised important issues about the public's view of the proper role of the BBC in its reporting of the conflict. Early on, a large majority (80%) believed that the BBC should reflect the full range of opinions about a situation, and a small majority took the view that the BBC should itself decide what information to give about the campaign. (Similarly 51% believed that the BBC did so decide). Later in the conflict, as the public's partisan position hardened, fewer now believed that it was right for the BBC to be even-handed editorially (down to 71%), and only about a third (31%) felt that the BBC should itself be deciding what information should be released. Clearly public support of the government's response to the crisis in general and of the Task Force in particular made it increasingly difficult for people at the same time to sustain their endorsement of broadcasters' traditional editorial independence.

Table 1:   Daily Average TV News Audiences, 1st and 2nd Quarters 1982

Source: BARB   % of UK population aged 4+ viewing in 1982

	Quarter 1	Quarter 2	Change Q.1 - Q.2 as % of Q.1 audience
<u>BBC1</u>			
Mon-Fri			
News Afternoon (12.30-1.00)	3.1	3.3	+6%
Early Evening News	16.9	14.3	-15%
Nine O'Clock News	16.2	18.4	+14%
Saturday			
Early Evening	17.1	16.5	-4%
Late Evening	20.4	18.8	-8%
Sunday			
Mid-day	6.6	4.5	-32%
Early Evening	18.7	11.5	-39%
Late Evening	6.0	15.5	+158%
<u>BBC2</u>			
Mon-Fri			
Mid Evening	3.7	3.1	-16%
Newsnight	2.0	3.0	+50%
Saturday			
Early Evening	2.3	2.6	+13%
Late Evening	2.9	3.6	+24%
Sunday			
Mid-Evening (Review)	2.1	6.0	+186%
<u>ITV</u>			
Mon-Fri			
News At One	6.2	5.7	-8%
Evening News	18.3	16.3	-11%
News At Ten	16.7	15.6	-7%
Saturday			
Early Evening	16.0	12.5	-22%
Late Evening	20.6	16.1	-22%
Sunday			
Early Evening	12.3	10.6	-14%
Late Evening	23.5	22.3	-5%

Did news audiences rise during the Falklands conflict as a whole?

Many factors contribute to the size of audience for a specific TV programme. Of particular importance are time of day, time of year, the competing programmes on other channels and the audience size for the preceding or following programme (known as the inheritance or the anticipation factor). First, then, were news audiences higher than they had been earlier in the year? Table 1 shows the audience sizes for a range of news programmes during the first and second quarters of 1982, broadly corresponding to the period before and during the Falklands conflict (2). For some programmes the audiences were up - most spectacularly for BBC1's late evening news on Sunday (up 158%), and BBC's mid-evening news on Sunday (up 186%), but also BBC2's Newsnight (up 50%), and BBC1's Nine O'Clock News (up 14%). None of the ITV news programmes covered increased its average audience during the Falklands conflict compared with earlier in the year.

Clearly, judged by this criterion, the BBC performed better than ITV. But it would be wrong to conclude that ITV audiences were poor. Because of seasonality, it is to be expected that audiences to the news on ITV and on BBC1 will decline as the year progresses; this certainly happened in 1981. Comparing the period April - June with January - March, audiences to ITV news bulletins were relatively higher between April and June 1982 than they had been in 1981; for some bulletins the decrease was less - for example, in 1982 the average audience to News at Ten was only 7% down between April and June compared with January to March 1982, whereas it had been 17% down in 1981 between the same two periods.

Overall, on weekdays, most news bulletins on BBC1 and ITV show increases or reduced decreases in audience size between the first and second quarters compared with 1981. The effect is marginally stronger for BBC1 than for ITV. The BBC1 Nine O'Clock News average audience actually increased between April and June and the 'Falklands Effect' can be represented as follows:

e.g. Small Expected Decrease

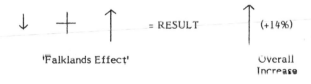

'Falklands Effect'   Overall
                           Increase

For News at Ten, which showed a decline in audience size, this would be:

Large Expected Decrease   Reduced
                                           Decrease

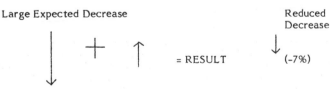

Weaker 'Falklands Effect'

As, therefore, one would expect to arise out of any major news 'event', a 'Falklands effect' is clearly evident in the higher than normal amounts of TV news viewing that occurred over the period of the conflict. The same comparison for a wider range of news programmes is shown in Table 2.

---

(2) A timetable of the key events in the Falklands Conflict is given in Appendix A.

Table 2: **% Change in average audience to selected news programmes between January–March and April–June**

	1981[3]	1982
BBC1		
Mon–Fri		
Early Evening News	−27	−15
Nine O'Clock News	− 4	+14
Saturday		
Early Evening	−34	− 4
Late Evening	−19	− 8
Sunday		
Midday	−46	−32
Early Evening	− 3	−39
Late Evening	− 7	+158
ITV		
Mon–Fri		
Evening News	−24	−11
News At Ten	−17	− 7
Saturday		
Early Evening	−21	−22
Late Evening	−15	−22
Sunday		
Early Evening	−55	−14
Late Evening	−44	− 5

BBC2 audiences appear largely unaffected by any possible Falklands effect – they show an increase in both 1981 and 1982. One notable exception is News Review, which showed a three-fold increase in audience. This might be a reflection of the week-long perspective of this particular programme, possibly providing a resume of events which were often, when first reported, incomplete or confusing.

---

(3)   These trends for 1981 are derived from audience sizes based on BBC's Daily Survey of Listening and Viewing, the method used by the BBC to measure audience size at that time. Estimates of audience sizes cannot be directly compared with those from BARB, but a comparison of trends is in order.

Table 3:   **% Change in average audiences between January-March and April-June**

	1981	1982
BBC2		
Mon-Fri		
Mid Evening	+17	-16
News Night	+44	+50
Saturday		
Early Evening	+33	+13
Late Evening	+33	+24
Sunday		
Mid Evening	+40	+186

Changes in scheduling, new programmes, and the strength of the competition will all, inevitably, have contributed to these trends on BBC and ITV. A plausible case has been made by Wober (4) that the inheritance factor accounts for the audience size of each of the main news bulletins. What he does not consider, however, is the extent to which the audience was tuned to the preceding programme because the news followed, rather than stayed on to see the news which happened to follow the preceding programme. The issue remains unresolved.

It is however inescapable that taking the three months as a whole, the Falklands Factor did affect the audience sizes for both BBC and ITV news programmes, and was stronger for BBC than for ITV.

---

(4)   The Falklands: Some Systematic Data on viewing behaviour and attitudes concerning television coverage of the conflict. IBA July 1982.

Chart 1: **Weekly Average Audiences For Main News Programmes, Weeks 8 to 30, 1982**

(Monday to Friday 9 O'clock News/News at 10; Saturday and Sunday Late Evening News BBC1/ITV)

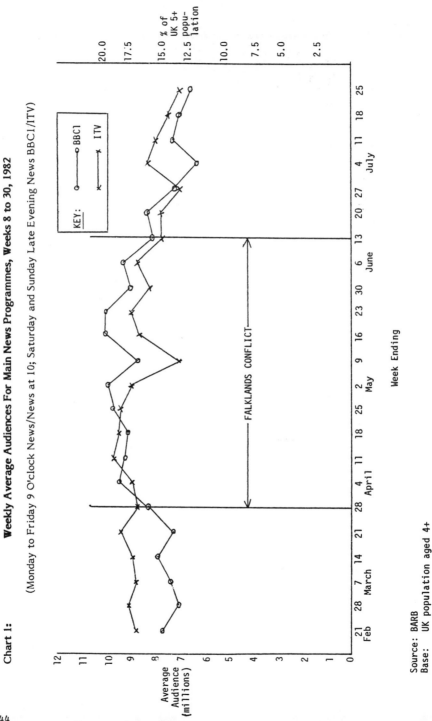

Week Ending

Source: BARB
Base: UK population aged 4+

What happened to audiences over shorter periods of time?

So far, we have discussed audience sizes for the Falklands conflict as a whole. The graph (facing) charts weekly average audiences for the main evening news bulletins on BBC1 and on ITV. In the short term, there were large gains in audience size for both channels. By the end of the conflict, however, both had declined from their respective peaks, but BBC's 9 O'Clock News declined more slowly than ITV's News At Ten - further evidence for a pro-BBC element in the overall effect of the Falklands conflict on TV news audiences.

The graph clearly indicates weeks of particular interest and those of less interest to the viewing public. Individual news bulletins did, indeed, attract large audiences - most dramatically, 17.25 million people saw ITV's news at 8.45 on Sunday 25th April, and 14.05 million saw BBC1's news at 9.30 on Thursday 27th May.

However, it is not the case that the vast majority of the public watched the main news bulletins or that the level of interest, as reflected in viewing figures, was maintained to the end of the conflict (15th June).

Table 4:

Consumption of News on One Day

	Date	Number of main news b'casts(1)	% of population (4+) seeing at least one	Average number seen out of 5
PRE-CONFLICT	22nd March	5	47	1.3
	26th March	5	46	1.2
	1st April	5	43	1.2
	2nd April	5	51	1.2
	5th April	5	50	1.3
	6th April	5	50	1.3
	14th June	5	45	1.3
	15th June	5	47	1.3
POST CONFLICT	5th June	5	42	1.3

(1)   Included in the analysis were

BBC1   Early Evening News
       9 O'Clock News

BBC2   Early Evening News

ITV   Early Evening News
       News At Ten

Were individuals watching more news bulletins?

Audiences to news programmes were higher during the Falklands conflict than otherwise might have been the case. What did this mean for the average viewer in terms of his or her likelihood of catching at least one of the five main news broadcasts on a particular day? Overall, although more people did see some news on television during the conflict than immediately before or after it, on any day around half the population (aged 4 or over) did not see any of the main news bulletins on TV. (Table 3). Immediately before the invasion, on an average weekday just under half saw at least one of the five main news bulletins (5).

In the days after the invasion this rose to half, a fairly marginal increase of a few percentage points. By mid-June, however, reflecting the decline in audiences noted above, the number of people who saw one of these five bulletins was back where it had been before the conflict started.

Further, there is no evidence of a voracious appetite for news during the period. Before the conflict viewers saw on average around 1.2/1.3 of these five bulletins each weekday. Even during the early days of April, this figure did not increase, and it remained steady into the summer. So, although on any day slightly more people were watching a news bulletin on television during the conflict, each viewer was not watching more news bulletins on any one day. However, over a longer period of time - all five weekdays - not only were slightly more people likely to see TV news at all, but (during the early part of the conflict) viewers were watching more news bulletins.

Between 22nd and 26th March, for example, just under two in five (38%) of the population (aged 4 or over) saw at least one edition of ITV's News At Ten. In the first week after the invasion, this rose to 40%, but fell back at the end of the conflict - to 38%. Over the same period, the average number of bulletins of News At Ten seen by each viewer in a week rose from 1.7 to 1.9 and fell back to 1.7 by mid-June. For BBC1's Nine O'Clock News, the increase in viewers over a week was even greater, and more sustained, lasting into June, but the average number of news bulletins seen rose only marginally.

---

(5)   Defined as BBC1's Early Evening News and Nine O'Clock News. BBC2's Early Evening News, ITV's Early Evening News and News At Ten.

Table 5:   **Consumption of news over five days**

Date	Number of news bulletins		% of population (4+) seeing any over 5 days		Average number seen out of 5	
22-29 March	5	BBC 9 O'Clock News	41		1.7	
	5	ITV News At Ten		38		1.7
5-9 April	5	BBC 9 O'Clock News	44		1.8	
	5	ITV News At Ten		40		1.9
14-18 June	5	BBC 9 O'Clock News	46		1.6	
	5	ITV News At Ten		38		1.7
5-9 July	5	BBC 9 O'Clock News	37		1.5	
	5	ITV News At Ten		38		1.7

Such increases in audience are important and indicate a heightened interest in the news during the Falklands conflict. But they do indicate only small shifts in people's behaviour, with a slightly increased tendency to view at all, and a marginal increase in the frequency of viewing.

Did people turn to the BBC?

Throughout the discussion above, the fact that the BBC attracted larger audiences than ITV has been noted. To recap:

Over the three months
- audiences to BBC news programmes showed greater increases than expected in comparison with ITV;

- audiences to BBC's 9 O'Clock News held up better over time than did those to ITV's News At Ten.

In addition, as Wober has demonstrated, the 9 O'Clock News was more likely than News At Ten to attract an audience significantly greater, and less likely to command an audience significantly smaller than the preceding programme. Whatever the appeal of the news, it was clearly greater for BBC than for ITV.

Not only did the public tend to support the BBC in their viewing, but also in what they said. In mid-May, in a special survey (6), 89% of adults said they had tuned to BBCTV to find out what was happening in the Falklands compared with 79% for ITV, and 39% said the BBC had given the best coverage of the crisis, compared with 30% for ITV.

---

(6)   For details of survey see next section.

The public's opinions of TV coverage

During April and early May, there was mounting controversy about the BBC's coverage of the Falklands conflict. In particular, there were accusations that the BBC reporting did not identify sufficiently strongly with the British cause. The Sun accused the BBC of treachery, a view shared by The Mirror and The Guardian. A Times leader on 13th May described the way 'the Government and others who have been outraged by some of the coverage, especially on the BBC, are afraid of national morale being sapped by too much prominence being given to Argentine propaganda, and by a degree of detachment on the part of some broadcasters that has been interpreted as according the same weight to the Argentine as to the British cause.'

In order to investigate the public's attitudes about these issues, a special survey was conducted on behalf of the BBC by Audience Selection Limited, among a sample of 1,049 adults interviewed by telephone on 13th May 1982. Following the cessation of hostilities, 533 of this sample were reinterviewed to establish the extent and nature of any changes in the public's reactions to the coverage of the conflict in general and to the BBC's coverage in particular.

In mid-May, the vast majority thought that BBCTV and ITV had each done a good job, with ITV marginally ahead (92% compared with 87% for BBCTV). Opinion was moderately rather than extremely enthusiastic, with significantly more people describing the coverage as 'fairly good' than as 'very good'. There was, however, some criticism of the BBC; one in ten said BBCTV's coverage was bad, compared with only 4% for ITV.

On the key issue of the amount of information about the British and Argentinian points of view, the BBC was criticised by around one in three for not giving enough information about the British point of view and by the same number for giving too much information about the Argentinian point of view. Although there were some complaints about the opposite - too much about the British and not enough about the Argentinian point of view - these were at a much lower level. So while there existed considerable support for the balance achieved by the BBC in its coverage, there was a significant minority feeling that the balance was wrong:

Table 6:	British point of view	Argentinian point of view
Base = all who saw BBC TV or heard BBC radio		
% who said that BBC is giving .... about .... point of view	%	%
Too much	13	34
Not enough	30	18
About right	54	44
Don't know	4	4
	100	100

One particularly controversial issue concerned whether, in the absence of British film about the Task Force, the BBC should have shown Argentinian film. The heated arguments in the press were reflected in the public's response, which was equally divided, with 45% of the view that the BBC should show Argentinian film and 47% that, in the absence of British film, no film should be shown. The public's views, therefore, reflected the controversy.

The issue of government control of the media and the independence of the BBC were investigated by asking two questions - first, whether the BBC or the government actually does decide what information to put out about the conflict, and, second, which should decide. On both counts the BBC was a more popular choice than the government, but around one in three thought the government did decide and the same number (but not necessarily the same people) that the government should decide.

Table 7:

Base = all respondents	Does decide	Should decide
% saying ... does/should decide	%	%
BBC	51	55
Government	32	34
Both	8	-
Neither	*	1
It depends	3	7
Don't know	6	3
	100	100

(* = less than 0.5%)

There was, however, overwhelming support for the BBC in the way it had covered the crisis; 81% of those interviewed said the BBC had behaved in a responsible manner, and only 14% that it had not; 5% did not know. This is reflected in the widespread view that the BBC should in the current situation (i.e. the Falklands conflict) pursue its traditional policy of reflecting the full range of opinions about a situation - 81% agreed that it should, 10% said it should not. The others either said the BBC generally failed to reflect situations, or did not know. It is clear that, while some were unhappy about the balance of coverage given to the British and the Argentinian points of view, this did not undermine the public's basic confidence in the BBC's handling of the situation.

What was the effect on public attitudes of the subsequent coverage of the crisis and the comparative absence of public criticism in the media of the BBC's handling of the crisis?

By the time hostilities had ceased, in many respects, public opinion had improved, in part undoubtedly reflecting a favourable reaction to the bearer of the good news of a British victory. There was a more widespread belief that the BBC had done a 'very good' job (up from 36% to 55%); and that the BBC had behaved in a responsible manner (up marginally from 81% to 84%). In spite of a better impression of the amount of information about the British and the Argentinian points of view there remained some doubts about the balance of coverage:

Table 8:	British point of view	Argentinian point of view
Base = all who saw BBC TV or heard BBC radio		
% who said that BBC is giving .... about .... point of view	%	%
Too much	10	23
Not enough	20	16
About right	64	53
Don't know	6	8
	100	100

More importantly, subsequent events and publicity about the role of the Ministry of Defence in releasing information about the Falklands seem significantly to have influenced the public's opinions about the role the BBC had adopted and the extent of government control of the media in the Falklands crisis, and, potentially of even greater significance, about the proper role of the BBC:

- There was a reduction in the number who felt that the BBC should pursue its traditional policy of reflecting the full range of opinions about a situation (down from 81% to 70%).

- The number who believed the BBC did decide for itself what information to put out declined and the number believing the government decided increased to a level significantly above that of the BBC:

Table 9: Base = all respondents	May	June
% who said .... does decide what information to put out	%	%
BBC	51	31
Government	32	41
Both	8	14
Depends	3	4
Don't know	6	11
	100	100

- There was a decline in the belief that the BBC should decide what information to put out (from 55% to 45%) though the increase in the number thinking that the government should decide was smaller (up from 34% to 38%). While there were still more people, therefore, believing that the BBC rather than the government should decide what information to put out about the Falklands crisis, unlike in mid-May, this was no longer the majority view.

There appears, therefore, to be an increasing discrepancy between the generalised confidence in the BBC and support for its handling of the crisis on the one hand, and beliefs about the independence of the BBC and the extent to which it is subject to government interference on the other. Clearly the Falklands represented a highly unusual situation, in which there was a large amount of media coverage of the issue of media independence and Ministry of Defence control of the supply of information to the media. It is possible that the public's response reflects these factors and that opinions will revert to pre-Falklands levels over time. On the other hand, it is also possible that the public debate about control of the media may for some time affect the public's expectations about television news and their confidence in and support for the independence of the media.

APPENDIX 1

TIMETABLE OF MAIN EVENTS IN
FALKLANDS CONFLICT 1982

April   2nd   Argentina invaded Falkland Islands.

12th   British naval blockade of Falklands begun.

25th   Reported that British forces had landed on South Georgia.

28th   Britain announced Total Exclusion Zone around the Falklands from 30th.

29th   Argentina declared 200 mile War Zone around Falklands, South Georgia and Sandwich Islands.

May   1st   Airborne assaults started on Port Stanley and Goose Green.

3rd   Argentine cruiser General Belgrano announced to have been hit by torpedoes on 2nd May.

4th   HMS Sheffield hit by Argentinian Exocet Missile. 20 officers and men died.

6th   Mrs. Thatcher expressed concern over media coverage of the crisis.

10th   Conservative MPs signed a Commons Motion critical of the BBC following a Panorama programme.

14th   188 Argentine prisoners captured on South Georgia.
       Marines landed on Pebble Island, off West Falkland.

21st   British Forces landed at Port San Carlos.
       HMS Ardent hit and sank. 22 missing, presumed dead.

24th   HMS Antelope announced to have been sunk.

25th   HMS Coventry attacked. 20 men killed.
       Atlantic Conveyor set ablaze. 9 men killed.

28th   Offensive to recapture Port Darwin. Attack on Goose Green.

June   1st   Announced that 250 Argentinians and 17 Britons died in battle for Port Stanley and Goose Green.

8th   HMS Plymouth, Sir Galahad and Sir Tristran attacked and damaged by Argentinian Air Force.

15th   Surrender document signed.

4. APPETITE FOR BREAKFAST TELEVISION

A pre-broadcast study of awareness and interest
July - December 1982
Rosemary Bristow, Senior Researcher (Special Projects)

Introduction

Six thirty on a winter's morning, January 17, 1983, saw a new arrival in British broadcasting - breakfast television in regular helpings. 'Breakfast Time' on BBC1 Mondays to Fridays from 6.30 to 9 am beat its commercial rival, TV-am, to the screen by a fortnight. Hosted by three presenters working in pairs - Frank Bough, Selina Scott and Nick Ross - the programme aimed to create an atmosphere of freshness and relaxation in which to provide a palatable diet of news, information, orientation and entertainment, on a rolling basis but within a clearly signalled, daily pattern.

Though 'Breakfast Time' was the first, regular, early morning television in Britain aimed at the general public, there had been other, more specialised, dawn telecasts. Open University had been broadcasting for some years; major news stories, including elections and space exploits, had been covered; special programmes were mounted for outstanding events such as a Royal wedding or the Papal visit. There had also been isolated local experiments with formats for a more permanent breakfast television service - nine weeks in 1977 in the Yorkshire-Tyne Tees ITV region, of news, cartoons and Peyton Place; or a week's 'radiovision', a televised version of BBC Radio Scotland's 'Good Morning Scotland' in December 1980.

Breakfast television on a more permanent basis arose out of the challenge issued by the IBA when, in January 1980, it invited tenders for a national, early morning service on ITV. The contract, to supply television programmes seven days a week between 6am and 9.15am, 'primarily, but not exclusively, of news, information and current affairs', was won by Peter Jay's TV-am, with its 'mission to explain' the daily news and its background, helped by a formidable team of television stars as the presenters. Those who were to remain with the company until its launch - David Frost, Angela Rippon, Anna Ford, Michael Parkinson and Robert Kee - were dubbed the 'Famous Five'.

Initially, there were BBC fears that such an array of stars and a concentration on news, information and features on ITV would threaten early morning radio audiences, particularly to Radio 4. Broadcasting Research Department was therefore asked to assess public interest in breakfast television and its likely impact on listening patterns. The results of a nationwide survey of adults, published in March 1981 (1), showed widespread indifference, or even opposition, to the general idea of breakfast television. Greatest enthusiasm came from already heavy viewers, from the young and from those with a working class, and less educated, background. Radio 1 and ILR seemed most at risk, not the more serious, information-orientated services. The potential audience for breakfast television wanted news, but 'entertainment' was also a major requirement.

For at least a year there was uncertainty as to whether the BBC would provide any breakfast television, or if they did, what form it would take. Eventually, in March 1982, the BBC announced the start, in early 1983, of a two and a half hour weekday service on BBC1.

---

(1)   BRD: 'Breakfast Television: The potential market and likely shift from morning radio to television' (VR/81/19).

Aims of the Research Programme

When the research programme was initiated, it was expected that breakfast television on BBC 1 would begin in January or early February 1983. The research aimed to examine the climate for breakfast television in the six months leading up to its expected start, then to monitor its impact. This paper deals only with studies carried out before the launch of Breakfast Time on 17 January 1983. Research carried out after the start of breakfast television will be reported separately.

The pre-broadcast investigations were planned to meet the following broad aims:

1.   To find out who is available to watch television on weekdays before 9.30am, what they are currently doing and how they feel at this hour;

2.   To establish how many TV sets people have and where they keep them;

3.   To track growth in public awareness of breakfast television;

4.   To assess the acceptability of breakfast television as a concept, as well as reaction to proposed items and presenters;

5.   To explore areas of resistance to breakfast television and the conditions under which reluctant viewers would watch.

Research Methods

A combination of desk research, field surveys and group discussions was used in the pre-broadcast studies.

1.   <u>Desk research</u>

   This aimed to bring together relevant material already available on people's behaviour in the early mornings, their attitudes, tastes and listening and viewing habits. To these ends, attention was paid to the following sources:

   1.1   Availability studies: who is at home and awake during each half hour between 6.00 and 9.30 am; (2)

   1.2   Listening and viewing at these times; (3)

   1.3   Previous surveys on set ownership and on attitudes and reactions to breakfast television. (4)

---

(2)   The People's Activities, 1974-75.   Published BBC Audience Research Department, 1978.

(3)   Estimates of audience size;
BRD's Daily Survey of Listening and Viewing, 1981.

BARB, January - December, 1982.

BRD Daily Survey of Listening, January - December 1982.

(4)   'Good Morning Scotland' January, 1981 (BRD,VR/81/19)

'Public Interest in Breakfast Time Television', August 1981, (MORI).

At the same time, a close check was kept on press coverage of breakfast television, relating publicity to general awareness of the coming services.

2. Field Surveys

Questions relating to breakfast television were added to three Omnibus surveys carried out by BRD in July, September and December 1982 (5). These were interviewer surveys with representative, quota samples of just over 1,000 adults aged 16 or over throughout the United Kingdom.

The questions were usually fairly simple, with pre-coded answers, though some open-ended questions were included. They covered issues such as:

- TV set ownership and location;

- awareness of breakfast television, the channels and dates when the services were expected to begin;

- intention to view and at what times;

- reasons for expecting never to watch, and the conditions under which resistance might be overcome;

- reaction to potential presenters and items on breakfast television (a changing list depending on specific interest).

3. Group discussions

'Potential breakfast viewers', generously interpreted as people not dismissing the idea of ever watching breakfast television in the future, were brought together in October 1982 in four small groups of 7 to 11 people to discuss the subject. In the same month, two supplementary, briefer discussions were arranged with people not specifically recruited as possible breakfast viewers.

The group discussions were intended to throw light on the family environment early in the morning and to understand how breakfast television might fit in with people's lives at this time of the day. The aim was to explore both activities and moods. In the light of both television and personal availability, as well as of expectations of the future service, who would be most likely to watch and how would they respond to the probable ingredients in BBC1's breakfast broadcasts?

---

(5)   Survey dates: Omnibus 13 5th-27th July, 1982

Omnibus 14 23rd September - 6th October, 1982

Omnibus 15 3rd - 14th December, 1982

Table 1 **Proportions of UK population aged 5+ at home and active on weekdays, 6.00–9.30am**

am	At home	At home and up	Listening to any radio
	%	%	%
6.00 - 6.30	97	7	2
6.30 - 7.00	95	16	4
7.00 - 7.30	90	32	11
7.30 - 8.00	82	49	24
8.00 - 8.30	71	55	20
8.30 - 9.00	47	37	1/
9.00 - 9.30	38	32	15

Source: BBC Audience Research Department: 'The People's Activities: Winter 1975'.

Table 2 **Early morning weekday activities among UK population aged 5+**

	6.30 – 7.00 am	7.30 – 8.00 am	8.30 – 9.00 am
	%	%	%
All listeners	4	24	17
of whom listening is the MAIN activity	6	5	7
Other activities:			
In bed	13	7	3
Getting up	42	33	11
Preparing food	10	15	13
Eating	14	21	14
Housework	3	4	15

Source: 'The People's Activities: Winter 1975'

Research Findings

1.   Influences relevant to breakfast viewing

Whether or not people in Britain take notice of, become interested in or even addicted to breakfast television is dependent on a wide range of influences -physical, social and psychological. Making a prediction about whether or not one would watch something quite new in one's experience requires the ability to assess one's life-style and that of the family, the flexibility to amend ingrained habits and one's expectations of what the television services are likely to provide. Questions are inevitably raised about how busy people are in the mornings, how they feel in terms of mood, alertness, and tolerance of perhaps an added distraction; whether they feel guilt about wasting precious time; what effect television in the morning might have on the rest of the family; even whether they are at home and able to watch at the time of transmissions.

1.1   Availability and morning activities

Are people home and can they afford the time to watch breakfast television? The BBC report 'The People's Activities' detailed the behaviour of the UK public aged five and over in 1974/1975. We are interested in what was happening on weekdays between 6am and 9.30am. Table 1 illustrates that though in Winter 1975 almost everyone was at home before 7am, few were up. Even fewer were listening to the radio. Between 7.30 and 8.30am came the peak time for being available at home and listening. After this, the potential home audience dropped sharply.

Before 9am 37% listened to any radio, the dominant stations being Radio 1, Radio 2 and ILR. But morning listening was very much a secondary activity to the demands of getting ready for the day, as Table 2 indicates.

1.2   TV set ownership and location

What about availability of the television in the morning? Where is it kept? Radio listening can more easily accompany the busy round of activity before leaving home or cleaning the house simply because radios are more portable and people tend to have more of them than TV sets. A survey in 1980 (6) of where people spent at least five minutes each morning before 9 o'clock showed - not surprisingly - the kitchen, bathroom and bedroom to be the most used rooms in the house (Table 3). It was then fairly rare to have a TV set in any of these places. Though almost all homes had a set in the living room, only 29% of adults over fifteen spent at least five minutes of their morning there. Another interesting finding from the same study was that over a third (38%) of adults said they never breakfasted at home. The impression gained is one of rush and of not being near a TV set in the mornings.

---

(6)   MORI: 'Public interest in Breakfast Time Television', 1980

Table 3   **Location of people aged 16+ and their TV sets**

	Spend 5 minutes or more before 9.00 am (1)	TV set location		
		Any (1) (Aug '80)	Main set (2) (Dec '82)	Other set(s) (2) (Dec '82)
Kitchen	69	3	1	6
Bathroom	58	-	-	-
Own bedroom	50	9	-	21
Living room	29	94	96	2
Dining room	12	6	2	4
Other bedroom	6	5	-	14
Breakfast room	6	1	NA	NA
Other room	NA	NA	1	3

Source: (1) MORI: 'Public Interest in Breakfast Television' 1980

(2) BRD Omnibus 15, December 1982

However, multi-set television ownership has since grown. By December 1982, 44% of adults interviewed on a BBC survey had two or more sets in their household (7). Additional sets were mainly in bedrooms - either adults' or children's. The kitchen was still an uncommon location. Portable sets had also increased, so that by the end of 1982, 44% of adults said they had one. The climate for watching television in the mornings was improving in terms of set ownership and location, but would habits change? Peter Bowman, an advocate of breakfast television, argued at the start of 1982 that there was no reason why people should spend time in their living rooms in the mornings in front of blank television screens (8). But what happens when the screen is not blank, and how do people feel about viewing early in the day?

1.3   Early morning viewing

Although the rival breakfast television services offered by Breakfast Time and TV-am were new to the British scene as 'permanent' features, there had been previous occasions on which programmes had been shown in the early mornings in the UK. These ranged from the regular Open University broadcasts to special news reports (notably during the Falklands campaign), reports of exceptional events such as election results, Royal weddings, the Papal visit to Britain and limited forays into breakfast television itself.

---

(7)   Omnibus 15, December 1982.

(8)   Peter Bowman: 'A Masius view of breakfast TV' in Media World, January 1982.

Table 4   Awareness of channels for breakfast television

	July 82 (1,086)	Sept/Oct 82 (1,101)	Dec 82 (1,141)
	%	%	%
BBC	13	10	17
ITV	14	17	19
Both	29	22	33
Other	NA	NA	1
Don't know	49	49	27
No TV/no reply	3	2	3
	___	___	___
	100	100	100

Source: BRD Omnibus surveys 13, 14, 15

Table 5   Awareness of starting date for breakfast TV on BBC1

	July 82 (1,086)	Sept/Oct 82 (1,101)	Dec 82 (1,141)
	%	%	%
July-Sept 82	5	NA	NA
Oct-Dec 82	12	20	NA
Dec 82	NA	NA	3
Jan-March 83	17	14	42
April 83 or later	19	8	15
Don't know	44	56	38
No TV/no reply	3	2	2
	___	___	___
	100	100	100

Source: BRD Omnibus surveys 13, 14, 15

Their impact on the British public varied, from very little for educational broadcasts and brief, unscheduled news bulletins, despite the highly charged, topical subject matter, to sizeable audiences for well-publicised and outstanding national and historic events. Open University transmissions and the Falklands news reports drew no more than 200,000 viewers on weekdays, usually less (9). At the other extreme, the Royal wedding in July 1981, a 'once-in-a-lifetime' event on a national holiday, was watched on average by 18 million people between 8 and 10am (10). More modest, but still impressive, were early morning audiences of 3.2 million watching the Pope's first visit to Britain (11). This was on a normal weekday, as was the long-awaited lifting of the 'Mary Rose'. Just under 3 million were following this historic broadcast between 9 and 9.30am (12).

Specific attempts to provide a breakfast television service were more difficult to assess. The hour-long weekday experimental schedule of news, cartoons and serial run for nine weeks in Yorkshire mainly attracted children in their school holidays (13).

BBC Scotland's five day 'radiovision' experiment of simultaneously televising and broadcasting the radio breakfast programme 'Good Morning Scotland' was seen, on average, by 2% of the population of Scotland (14). Though hailed as a success, the experiment was not repeated. Finally, a more concerted effort to provide breakfast telecasts, this time nationally, was BBC1's Breakfast with Brisbane. Over seven days in October 1982, these live and recorded transmissions from Australia of the Commonwealth Games averaged one million viewers a day between about 8 and 8.45am (15).

Though there is some evidence that Britons were prepared to make an effort to watch notable telecasts early in the morning, whether either adults or children would watch everyday breakfast television on normal school or working days was more open to question.

---

(9)   BARB, 1982.

(10)   Daily Survey of Listening and Viewing, 29th July 1981.

(11)   BARB, 28th May 1982.

(12)   BARB, 11th October 1982.

(13)   Harry Henry: 'Breakfast Television: much ado about remarkably little' in ADMAP, October 1981, p 491.

(14)   Daily Survey of Listening and Viewing, 1st - 5th December 1980.

(15)   BARB, 3rd - 9th October, 1982.

1.4   Morning mood and social environment

Given that people are prepared to make an effort in the mornings to watch the unusual on television - whether for its novelty or its inherent interest and importance - what is likely to happen on a day to day basis? The impression gained from the group discussions was that although people were clearly influenced in their expectations of watching by how busy they felt they were in the mornings, this was not the sole criterion. Also important were personal mood and perceived flexibility or willingness to adapt, among other factors.

Mood seemed to vary with the individual's physical make-up or ease of waking up and feeling alert, with the activities of the night before and of the day ahead, and with the weather. One faction craved peace and quiet in the mornings; they would rather sleep or read the paper than watch television. Slow wakers felt that breakfast television would be acceptable provided it was relaxing and soothing. Others, in contrast, required stimulation to get them going in the mornings; this breed welcomed bright, lively, noisy programming. Yet others felt bowed down by poor weather or by boring jobs awaiting them at work or at home; they believed that cheering, 'uplifting' television output at the start of the day could dispel their gloom and cares.

Being 'in the right mood' for watching in the mornings, regardless of availability, is influenced by social conditioning and environment. For some viewers, television is seen as a reward for the day's work, its function to provide evening relaxation. Young mothers in the group discussions claimed they would be unable to concentrate on watching breakfast television because of noise and distraction from the children. Others felt guilt would prevent them from relaxing to watch television whilst housework remained undone or work or school awaited. A fairly common theme in both the group discussions and the Omnibus surveys was ambivalence over the attractions of television and its disruptive influence both on viewers themselves and their families.

Not all respondents showed ambivalence about breakfast television. Some were quite clear that they were not prepared to change their morning habits, either by getting up earlier to make time, in leaving home later or in reorganising activities around a television set. Yet those keen to watch were prepared to make these changes. Some group members predicted that turning on the television in the morning would become second nature, as it is with radio; that it would be on in the background for people to look at whenever they could spare a few minutes; and that people's lives would change to fit in with breakfast television.

To cope with these contrasting requirements it would seem that Breakfast Time, to be a success, would need to be bright, stimulating and optimistic without being too noisy and brash, to be helpfully informative and to be segmented in such a way so that it could be easily taken up and dropped by busy people.

2.   Awareness of breakfast television

Breakfast television was widely discussed in detail in the press in January and February 1983 immediately before, during and after the launch of two competing services. The subject also received close attention when TV-am won its contract at the end of December 1980 and when the BBC announced its forthcoming service in March 1982. But in the six months before the services actually began, what did Britain as a whole know about breakfast TV?

Very little, it seemed. Between July and December 1982, public awareness of the two services, either in terms of who would provide them, or when, was scant (Tables 4 and 5). By December 1982, more people were prepared to guess the channels and starting dates than in September or July, but even six weeks before Breakfast Time went on air, no more than one third of adults recognised the rival nature of the services. Only four out of ten correctly pinpointed the starting dates as between January and March 1983. Table 6 contrasts the kinds of viewer who were most and least knowledgeable about the forthcoming breakfast channels.

Table 6   Awareness or ignorance of channels to be used for Breakfast TV

Those thinking Breakfast TV will be on both BBC + ITV	% of group	Those replying 'don't know' which channel(s) Breakfast TV will be on	% of group
All viewers aged 16+	33	All viewers aged 16+	28
Awareness highest among:		Ignorance highest among:	
- 30-49 year olds	42	- very light viewers	40
- those completing education aged 17-19	41	- older people (aged 55+)	38
- BBC 1 + 2 viewers	40	- unskilled working class	33
- 16-34 year olds	38		
- those with children under 16	38		

Source: Omnibus 15, 3-14 December, 1982

Group discussions held in October 1982 revealed a confusion, at least in some minds, between breakfast television and Channel 4. Some people clearly believed them to be identical; a few others just assumed them to be the same. There was a lack of understanding about TV-am as a new national company located in London; it was taken for granted that ITV would, as usual, provide a regionally based service. There was also no clear appreciation that BBC and ITV would be broadcasting simultaneously. Group members concluded, on reflection, that if one channel began breakfast television, the other would soon 'follow suit'.

People in the group discussions were hazy about both the transmission times for breakfast television and the presenters. Four of the 'Famous Five' - Anna Ford, Angela Rippon, Michael Parkinson and David Frost -were associated with breakfast TV, but were more likely to be linked with BBC TV than with ITV. There was even less awareness of the Breakfast Time presenters - not surprisingly, as not all had been appointed by then, let alone publicly announced.

Public ignorance and confusion is understandable in the light of the start of other new television services and their attendant publicity. S4C in Wales and Channel 4 in the rest of UK were launched at the beginning of November, 1982 as the first new television outlets since the creation of BBC2, nearly twenty years earlier. Press coverage concentrated on these new services at least until they were on air. By early December 1982 it was obvious to many that Channel 4 did not broadcast at breakfast time. However, the publicity machine was still not heavily in gear, partly due to doubts whether union disputes would let either service start at all. It is therefore not surprising that the public should be unclear as to who would be broadcasting what, when, or where.

3.   Expectations of watching breakfast television

3.1   Viewers' expectations of watching

There is of course another explanation for the relatively low public awareness about breakfast television, and that is lack of interest. Is it at all relevant to anyone? Who is likely to watch? People's expectations of watching breakfast TV on either channel did not blossom as the starting dates drew nearer. The enthusiastic, who anticipated watching at least once a week on weekdays, were outweighed by less committed viewers and the 'wait and see' brigade, while over half (58%) the adult population rejected the idea of breakfast television (Table 7).

Table 7   **How often viewers expected to watch breakfast television on BBC1 on weekdays**

	July 82 (1,059)		Sept/Oct 82 (1,075)		Dec 82 (1,117)	
	%		%		%	
Every day	3		2		3	
Most days a week	5	15	5	13	6	15
At least once a week	7		6		6	
Less than once a week	2		1		1	
Hardly ever	17	19	19	20	15	16
Never	56		58		58	
Depends	9		7		9	
Don't know/no reply	1	10	2	9	2	11
TOTAL	100		100		100	

Source: BRD Omnibus Surveys 13, 14, 15, 1982

The channel providing the service made no difference. The same pattern of awareness was found for both BBC and ITV.

Table 8   **Kinds of viewer expecting to watch, or never watch, Breakfast TV**

Viewers expecting to watch Breakfast TV on BBC 1 'at least once a week'	% of group	Viewers expecting 'never' to watch Breakfast TV on BBC 1	% of group
All viewers aged 16+	15	All viewers aged 16+	58
Viewing Breakfast TV most likely among:		Viewing Breakfast TV most likely among:	
- 16-29 year olds	25	- light viewers (less than 17 hours per week)	70
- heavy viewers (over 31 hours per week)	23	- upper middle class	64
- those with children aged 0-4 in household	22	- BBC 1 + 2 viewers	63
- Radio 1 listeners	22	- Radio2/Radio 4 listeners	63
- housewives, students + unemployed	19	- wide age range 35+	62
		- employed or retired	62

Source: Omnibus 15, 3-14 December 1982

3.2   Fluidity of viewing expectations

It should be remembered that by December 1982, relatively few people in Britain had watched early morning telecasts or had much idea of what to expect of breakfast television.   Their assessment of their future viewing was therefore somewhat provisional, based on their present activities and availability, their ability to imagine changes in their life-style and their beliefs about the eventual television service.   In these circumstances, 'never' is a relative term.   In September 1982, half the respondents on Omnibus 14 who expected not to watch breakfast television were able, under close questioning, to think of occasions when they might watch.   Admittedly, these depended on departures from the normal, either in their own lives or in the world at large. Illness, holidays or being away from work would provide the unaccustomed free time to watch.   Curiosity about a new, increasingly talked-about service had to be taken into account, while the occurrence of major, newsworthy - perhaps even historic - events were considered important enough to disrupt normal, workaday, morning activities.

This meant that about seven out of ten adults aged 16 or over, or about 30 million people, conceded that they would, or might, watch breakfast television at some point, given the right circumstances.   In terms of regular viewing, this reduced to about 6½ million adults believing they would watch 'at least once a week', and about one million, or 3% of adults, expecting to watch every day.

3.3   Who said they would watch?

What kinds of people were prepared to watch breakfast television?   Members of the group discussions thought it would be 'others' rather than themselves.   Those seeing themselves as future viewers more often were the older housewives over 50 or the retired, and the non-working, especially with young children.   'Others' envisaged as likely viewers encompassed a wide range of housebound people, shift-workers, 'office' workers, the young unemployed and children.   The Omnibus surveys produced fairly similar findings.   Table 8 illustrates the groups considering themselves most or least likely to watch.

Non-viewers tended to be upmarket, light viewers, aged over 35 and listening mainly to Radio 2 or Radio 4.   As in an earlier survey before TV-am won its franchise (16), this suggested that the average 'Today' listener, for example, would be fairly immune to the appeal of breakfast television.   However, half the 'never' group were able to imagine watching it at least on rare or special occasions.   Interested in immediate, visual coverage of outstanding news and sporting events, these people could occasionally be weaned across to breakfast TV.   They tended to be of higher social class and more educated than those rejecting breakfast TV outright.   Heavy viewers, older and lower working class adults figured more prominently among the hard-core resisters.   (Perhaps they find it more difficult to change their daily behaviour, or to imagine doing so).

Though habits may indeed have been altered when faced with the reality of breakfast television, the fact remains that even a few weeks before it started, not many people in Britain expected to make a practice of watching it.

---

(16)   BRD 'Breakfast Television' March 1981

4.   What to serve for breakfast?

4.1   General flavour

Intentions to watch breakfast television are tied up not only with availability and access
to a TV set, but also with expectations of what would be provided. In October 1980
(17), those interested in the prospect clearly favoured a mixture of entertainment and
news or information. This was borne out in group discussions with likely viewers in
October 1982. These revealed a desire for news and the kind of orientation to the day
already heard on radio, fleshed out with pertinent advice for people's daily lives. But
the primary request was for 'entertainment'. In general, the 1982 group discussions
suggested people wanted breakfast television to provide a lift to the day, to be light-
hearted and sunny and to avoid depressing news. Though a few in the groups wanted
soothing early in the morning, more preferred to be stimulated and amused.

Because of the nature of people's early mornings, participants wanted the items on
breakfast TV to be short and varied, with no more than ten minutes on any topic. No-
one wanted to be tied down to the TV set, but to be given 'bits and pieces' to overhear
and choose from. The ideal was conceived as a 'visual newspaper' - that is, tabloid -
with a variety of main news and 'human interest' or 'funny' news, gossip, cartoons,
topical items and horoscope. It was also imagined as a visual version of one's favourite
radio, almost regardless of station. These characterisations in terms of what is already
familiar may indicate people's difficulties in conceptualising something new.

There was, however, a certain cynicism expressed in the group discussions. It was
anticipated that breakfast television, when served, would be a heavier meal than was
wanted at that time of day.

4.2.   Palatability of the proposed ingredients

4.2.1. Breakfast television for a general audience

The three Omnibus surveys in July, September and December 1982 were used to test out
how welcome were various proposed items for breakfast television, and when to place
them on weekdays between 6 and 9.30 am. Interested viewers - that is, those who did
not rule out the possibility of watching at that time - were also asked for each half hour
whether or not they expected to watch breakfast television. The group discussions
allowed further exploration of material acceptable at breakfast time, as well as
suitable treatment of it.

---

(17)   BRD 'Breakfast Television' March 1981

Table 9

Breakfast TV items appealing to different groups within the potential audience

Item	% Very or quite interested	Sex M	Sex F	Age 16-24	25-34	35-44	45-54	55+	Class AB	C1	C2	DE	Employment F/T emp	H/wife	Retired	Other	Children in H/H 0-4	5-15	None
Regional news	83-91								-										
Local information	84				-														
What's going on in your region	82				-										+				
Regional weather forecasts	74				-														
Consumer advice	61					+						-							
Sports news	57	+	-																
Medical topics	55-57	-	+											+			+		
UK weather forecast	56			-															
National job scene	51	[--]	[++]					-							[--]	+			
Cooking	51	[--]	[++]																
Gardening	51						+	+						+	+	+			
Traffic reports	49			-		+			+				-		-				
Unusual world weather	47					+													
Keep fit	43	-	+				+	+	[-]	+									
Phone-in doctor	41	-							-										
Job finder service	39	[--]	+				+	[--]	-	-			-	+	[-]	[++]			
Phone-in to presenters	38																		
Thought for the day	38	-	[-]	-				[++]	-	-	+		+	+	-				
Daily recipe	34	[++]	[-]	+							-	+	[++]	+	+				
Diet advice	28	-	+										-	+	+				
Celebrity's recipe	27	-	+	-					-				-	+	-				

+ 10-19% above average
[++] 20+ above average
- 10-19% below average
[-] 20-% below average

SOURCE: Omnibus 13, 14, 15 (July, September, December 1982)

Widespread interest was shown by 'potential viewers' in regional news and local information. Such material presented no apparent problems for scheduling but depended for its success on the ability of the breakfast progamme to opt out regionally. As this was not feasible for TV-am, the provision of local news would give Breakfast Time on BBC1 a competitive advantage.

Other items, appealing to half or more of the interested audience, included consumer and medical advice, sports news, national weather forecasts, cooking, gardening and the national job scene. At the tail end of the list, of interest to only about a quarter of the possible viewers, were diet advice and recipes from celebrities. However, as Table 9 illustrates, certain items had a definite sectional appeal. It was important to identify the tastes of people available at different times during the breakfast period so that the various items could be included at the most suitable points in the programme.

4.2.2. Breakfast television for children

Questions added to BRD's Daily Survey of Listening and Viewing in October 1980 suggested whole-hearted support among 5-15 year olds for breakfast television, and a readiness by them to desert radio in its favour (18). The inclusion of items of possible interest to children on BBC1's Breakfast Time was therefore considered, though with caution. Mindful of accusations of generating family conflict at a critical time of the day, parental approval rather than child preferences was explored. All adults interviewed on Omnibus 14 in September 1982, who had parental responsibility for children under 16 in their households, were asked what they would allow their children to watch on breakfast TV. All five items in Table 10 seemed fairly acceptable to parents, especially children's news bulletins.

Table 10   **Acceptability to parents of children's items on breakfast television**

	% of parents approving
News bulletins especially for children	70
Help with homework	67
Cartoons	65
Keep fit exercises	60
Children's drama serials	57

Source: BRD Omnibus 14, September 1982

(18)   BRD 'Breakfast Television' March 1981

The subject of children and breakfast television dominated the groups which included parents or grandparents. Contrary to the Omnibus results, which suggested considerable parental support for informative, education-oriented material for children on breakfast television, fathers in the groups tended to separate school work and learning from early morning TV. Children, they felt, had a right to be entertained, not 'bludgeoned' with information; homework should be done in the evenings in a disciplined way, not just before school. Cartoons and drama serials may well be very popular with youngsters (the former with men too) but could lead to fights between children and parents over the need to get to school on time. Entertaining material for children was fine for those under school age or for those at home sick, it was argued, but in general should be kept for weekends and school holidays.

4.3.   Detailed opinions of the ingredients

The six group discussions contributed to an understanding of how the various items should be interpreted and presented.

4.3.1. National and regional news/information

Attitudes towards news on breakfast television were polarised, depending on age and radio preferences. The young (aged 16-30) who listened widely to Radio 1 and II R rejected news as boring; for them, news was either mentally shut out or was heeded if short, local and/or lightweight.

Older respondents, particularly those favouring Radio 4 or BBC local radio, welcomed news as essential for the day's start, especially for people not taking newspapers. However, they too warned against too much 'depressing' news, on the IRA, trade unions, politics or economic problems. There was a preference for extended local news rather than 'too much' repetition of the same, or updated, news.

Keen interest was expressed in having localised information on morning television, in parallel with local radio. It was thought ITV would provide better local coverage (though BBC TV was expected to do things better overall) because it was assumed that TV-am, like the other ITV companies, would be regionally based. However, Breakfast Time intended to fully exploit the BBC's network of regional centres, an advantage not easily open to its commercial rival.

4.3.2. Advice

Consumer advice, presented in the style of 'That's Life' or 'Watchdog', was commended as suitable for breakfast television. The researching and pursuit of 'cons' in a serious, tenacious fashion were appreciated, especially when placed in an overall entertaining setting. Requests were made not only for information on consumers' legal rights but also best buys for the day's shopping and on value for money in general.

Some of the women in the discussion groups passionately advocated the inclusion of advice on individuals' welfare rights and of a job finder service on breakfast television. If phone-ins on these subjects were to be introduced, they recommended that calls should come from ordinary members of the public and that great care needed to be taken with the choice of persons answering the calls. Sensitivity and accurate advice were the keynotes, to be dispensed by neither 'politicians' nor 'celebrities' out of touch with ordinary lives. On the suggestion of advertising either jobs or job hunters on early morning television, the young unemployed were more cynical, convinced that it raised false hopes and that they were still asleep then anyway.

4.3.3. Cooking/gardening/keep fit

These all appealed to women, though of different ages. There was a wide range of views as to how often cooking items or recipes should be shown on breakfast television, if at all. Some looked forward to ideas for the day's shopping or meals. Recipes needed to be economical and easy, pre-tested and pre-costed. They had to be suitable for the family, yet widen the taste horizons. Demonstrations were preferred.

Gardening - whether phone-ins, demonstrations of simple, light tasks (like planting bulbs), or escapist features on sunlit gardens - appealed to older women in the discussion groups.

Younger women were keen on the idea of daily, do-it-yourself keep fit, but questioned whether breakfast was the appropriate time, either to watch or participate. There seemed to be a preference for a good, half-hour workout, after the family had left for work or school. Interested women who went to regular keep-fit classes pointed out that exercises were more fun done in similar company than alone.

4.3.4. Entertainment

Both pop music and astrology appealed strongly as potential ingredients in breakfast television. Those under 30 wanted a cheerful background to 'jig about to' - a visual Radio 1 or ILR. Preferences were expressed for early morning concerts, pre-recorded videos and favourite performers. Interviews with pop stars or groups were of interest, depending on the performers involved, but were not acceptable as a replacement for music.

Working class housewives in the groups enjoyed the idea of a televised horoscope in the mornings. Though they saw it mainly as a 'female' amusement, there were hints that 'there's something in the stars'. The interested saw breakfast TV becoming an extension of their daily papers and insisted that they would watch a TV horoscope. Settling on an appropriate time of the morning for it was more difficult.

4.3.5. Other material

A wide variety of other kinds of material was suggested with emphasis on the entertaining, lively, funny, stimulating or practical. Highlights of evening television, especially sport, were recommended for shift workers.

4.3.6. People

Whether they were well-known or ordinary people, those appearing on the programme as guests or contributors were required to be really interesting in their own right. As regards presenters of breakfast TV, the qualities looked for by viewers were fairly similar to those wanted of the programme overall: liveliness, approachability, professionalism - and perhaps someone new to the screen.

Table 11   Kinds of people expecting to watch any breakfast television on weekdays, 6.00 – 9.30am

am	% all 'potential' viewers	Sex	Age	Class	Employment	Children under 15 in household
6.00 – 6.30	8	Men	45 – 54	C2	Full-time employed	None
6.30 – 7.00	12	→	↓	C2DE	→	None or aged 5-15
7.00 – 7.30	23	→ Men/Women	35 – 54	all	→	aged 5-15
7.30 – 8.00	30	Men/Women	→	AB or C2	Students F/T employed Unemployed	more with none
8.00 – 8.30	39	Women/Men	55+ or 25 – 34	C2	Unemployed Students Retired Housewives	aged 0-4
8.30 – 9.00	37	Women →	55+ →	C2DE	Housewives Retired P/T employed	aged 0-4 or none
9.00 – 9.30	40			DE	Housewives Retired Unemployed	→

Source: Omnibus 13, July 1982

5.   Scheduling

5.1.   Times breakfast viewers expect to watch

As already noted, some of the proposed items for breakfast television were popular with almost all the likely audience while others appealed to specific groups within the audience. The aim in scheduling the various items that would make up the $2\frac{1}{2}$ hours of Breakfast Time was to establish who was available at the different stages throughout the programme and to put on material suitable for that specific audience. Table 11 provides a rough sketch of the kinds of adult who, in July 1982, thought they might see some breakfast television on weekday mornings. The estimates are fairly generous and should probably be interpreted as 'times when I am up and about, and would watch if I had the time and it interested me'. Only the main sub-groups (with a higher than average presence) at each half hour have been listed though they are obviously not the only potential viewers available. Predictable patterns emerge, starting with a mainly male, working class, employed audience in the first hour covered from 6 - 7am. This gives way to a more mixed, general audience of adults and children, workers and non-workers, male and female, over a wide range of ages and class backgrounds. After 8am, full-time workers, men and school age children are gradually replaced in the next ninety minutes by part-time or non-working viewers, women and adults with pre-school children. The final hour is dominated by working class respondents, housewives and the retired, or mothers of young children. This represents a very approximate guide to the likely television audiences but indicates the likely composition of the audience at different times.

5.2.   The breakfast menu

Next came the task of matching up the items that some people were interested in seeing with the times at which they thought they would be watching. In essence, this involved placing material of greater interest to men, and particularly working class men, earlier in the morning; items with more middle class appeal towards the centre; and those particularly attractive to housewives or the elderly later in the programme. The suggested broad time-bands for different kinds of proposed breakfast material are outlined in Table 12.

Table 12   **Suggested times for Breakfast TV items**

Timeband (am)

6.00-6.30   6.30-7.00   7.00-7.30   7.30-8.00   8.00-8.30   8.30-9.00   9.00-9.30

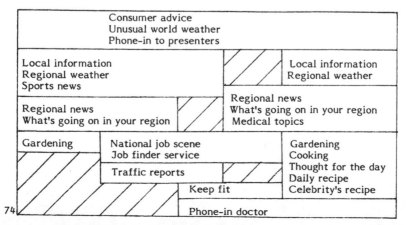

6.   Concluding remarks

The pre-broadcast research covered people's awareness of the approach of British breakfast television and how they responded to the idea of it. Despite occasional, atypical, early morning programmes on television, very few people had first-hand experience of 'breakfast television proper' nor had they formed very clear ideas of what to expect from the pre-publicity in the press. It is quite difficult for people not only to predict the content and format of a new type of television programme but also to conjure up the experience of watching television at an unfamiliar time of the day. Yet they were able to discriminate between offered items for breakfast television and, with encouragement in group discussions, could develop fairly coherent pictures of what they hoped the new services would provide.

News, both regional and national, information, helpful advice and entertainment were seen as the important ingredients in breakfast television, served in small doses in an informal, light-hearted manner. It is up to further research after the start of Breakfast Time and TV-am to determine whether these expectations have been met; whether even marginally interested viewers have been able to adjust their lives - and in what way - to make room for breakfast television; whether, in fact, breakfast TV becomes part of the national way of life.

Of particular interest will be the impact, if any, on early morning listening habits. Will breakfast viewers continue to listen to their normal early morning stations as well as watch television, or will they be wooed away? If so, which stations are most at risk? Or will viewers come from the ranks of non-listeners in the morning, thus extending the broadcast audience? After the start of breakfast television, a second set of research studies will be directed at answering such questions as these and at assessing the response of the public in Britain to the new breakfast services. These will be reported in a year's time.

5. DBS AND CABLE - THE CONSUMER'S VIEW

Pam Mills, Head of Special Projects

Background

During 1982 a number of developments occured which will arguably affect the whole structure of UK broadcasting by the end of the decade. Video ownership leapt from 4% to 15% of UK homes; there was a dramatic decline in TV viewing which was partly due to the use of video, but also seems to reflect a 'turn-off'. Both attracted a lot of media attention. But Cable and Direct Broadcasting by Satellite (DBS) attracted even more attention and debate. Conferences and Seminars abounded that gazed into a crystal ball about the new technology.

The Conservative Government clearly supported the cabling of the UK as a prerequisite for the post-industrial society, providing the infrastructure for comprehensive integrated communication systems in the 1990's and beyond, and activity and investment in key industrial sectors in the 1980's and beyond. The means to this end was to be entertainment - based Pay TV. In March, the report of the Information Technology Advisory Panel (ITAP) concluded that de-regulation deserved further study. The Hunt Committee, appointed in April, reported in October; its recommendations, basically very favourable to cable operators, included

- the creation of a formal and competitive franchising system;

- the creation of a new supervisory cable authority;

- income through a combination of basic service rental charges, premium service subscriptions and advertising/sponsorship revenue;

- existing and future BBC and IBA services must be carried on cable;

- no exclusive rights for national sporting events;

- ten year initial franchises for cable operators, eight years on renewal;

- no quotas on British material.

Experience of cable in the UK is limited in quality if not in quantity. Approximately 14% of homes - 2.7 million - are wired to cable systems. Over 1.6 million are connected to cable television systems covering entire towns or large areas of towns, known as Communal Antenna Television (CATV). The rest are connected to aerials shared by fewer homes -100 or less - known as Master Antenna Television (MATV). The systems themselves are, however, old and technically obsolete. Cable was originally developed mainly to combat poor reception and to prevent the proliferation of individual aerials on large housing developments. Most systems, therefore, are capable of transmitting only 4-6 channels of programming and will, therefore, need to be re-engineered if multi-channel Pay TV and all broadcast signals are to be carried.

The way seemed opened for a rapid development of cable.

At the same time, the BBC was negotiating with UNISAT with a view to providing programmes on two channels when the satellite comes into operation in 1986. So the BBC had an interest in developments from three points of view - as the country's major broadcaster, as the potential operator of a DBS service, and as the potential supplier of programmes to cable services - either direct or via DBS. In addition, the BBC had, in 1981, joined with Visionhire, the second largest cable system operator in the UK, to offer an experimental subscription service as one of 13 licenced by the Home Office. Showcable, showing mainly films, was available in parts of Inner London. This experiment offered the BBC some experience of operating a Pay TV system, but on a limited basis and only in one area, which was in many ways atypical of the country as a whole.

In such a developing situation, the BBC identified a need for a range of information on the potential market for its services, however defined. The recent US experience provided one model for development of cable. Over a relatively short period of time, one in five US homes had subscribed to Pay TV, and one in three homes were already cabled, yielding total cable revenues of over four billion dollars in 1982. But the US was quickly recognised as of possibly limited relevance to the UK market for several reasons - the UK's public service tradition and regulated entertainment; a generally higher standard of programming; less intrusive TV advertising; a lower interest in television, as reflected in the much lower hours per viewer in UK compared with the US; and, crucially, a healthy video market.

In order to provide a basis for projecting future demand for new programming services, delivered by cable or by DBS, the BBC itself undertook a number of projects and also bought into several syndicated studies, notably that produced by CIT in October 1982.

This paper will highlight some of the main findings to emerge from two of these research projects and point to some of their possible implications for the BBC.

CIT's Estimates for The Market for Cable in The UK

CIT (1) estimated that by 1992 25-40% of UK households will be linked to cable. Between 23-36% will subscribe to Multichannel Subscription TV, 21-31% will subscribe to a premium Pay TV service, and 5-10% to interactive systems and/or other applications. A basic assumption is that an area covering 80% of the population can be profitably cabled and that 60% of the population in these areas is able and prepared to pay -resulting in a maximum potential of around 50% of the population.

For the purpose of forecasting, the various scenarios assume a 22 channel cable system, operated on a two-tier basis, both tiers containing several channels, at a cost of £18 a year for the basic tier and £96 a year for the premium tier, plus a one-off £25 connection fee.

The higher estimate - of 40% by 1992 - assumes favourable conditions for ownership, connection and control of cable, and for advertising; long franchises; availability of BBC's DBS service for cable programming; interactive services and use of tree and branch coaxial cable (i.e. the cheapest option). The pessimistic estimate - of 25% - assumes two or three of the following - restricted advertising; a requirement for local switched optical fibre networks; no interactive services; and state monopoly of infrastructure. A major difference between these forecasts is the date at which cable starts to get off the ground. In the optimistic forecast a 1984 start date is assumed. If things do not start to move by 1984, a reassessment will have to be made by the late '80's, resulting in a more pessimistic outcome by 1992.

It is important to note the asssumption in these forecasts that in the early days a large part of the growth will come from recabling of existing cable systems or the provision of off-air broadcast service by an aerial and the use of their limited cable channels (usually 4-6) for subscription services. In the optimistic forecast, for example, by 1986, out of 17% of households subscribing to a multichannel service, the majority - 12% - were already linked to cable in 1982. The ease and speed with which these systems will be updated is, however, a matter for conjecture.

---

(1)   Cable TV Communications is Western Europe (CIT Research, November 1982)

Two major factors will affect the rate of development in the UK - DBS and video. Neither factor was present in the US. The impact of DBS could reduce the potential for cable. In the event of DBS becoming well established before cable, and offering attractive programming, the appeal of cable could be seriously diminished. Similarly, a healthy cable market would reduce the market for DBS. It is arguable whether satellite has potential as a means of direct delivery to the home but, in its optimistic scenario for UK, CIT assumes the availability of BBC satellite programming as a means of feeding cable systems, and ignores the possibility of a healthy market for satellite broadcasting direct to the home.

Video, unlike DBS, is already having an effect on television viewing and accounted for some of the apparent decline in TV viewing in late 1982 and early 1983. The projected 35% video ownership by 1985 will undoubtedly affect the uptake of cable, in that it restricts both the time and, perhaps more importantly, money available for video entertainment. Although video and cable can be complementary, for many households they will be viewed as alternatives, at least until the cost of acquiring them is reduced in real terms.

So, although many of the assumption in CIT's optimistic scenario may well materialise, timing will be crucial for the success of DBS and cable.

The Nature of The Market - CIT's Consumer Research

CIT's consumer research was based on three separate, but complementary samples. A lengthy and extensive interview was conducted with a sample of 543, representative of the UK population in households with television. A much shorter questionnaire, covering key questions, was used to interview an omnibus sample of 2,361 people, again representative of the UK population in households with TV. A special sample of 147 were interviewed, with the long questionnaire, in three Pay TV experiment areas. Fieldwork was carried out in mid-1982.

Asking members of the general public about their likely behaviour in unfamiliar hypothetical situations can produce very unreliable results and presents problems for projecting demand in any new market. In this case, estimates of the likely uptake of cable TV were derived in two ways

    i)   Indirectly: by examining behaviour in relation to, and attitudes to, leisure and television, in order to identify unsatisfied demand; and by scrutinising the characteristics of households to establish the feasibility of subscription (i.e. could they afford it?).

    ii)   Directly: by establishing the level of interest in various programming options.

In both approaches, interpretation of the response to what appear to be very simple and potentially dangerous questions requires a high level of experience and sophistication. For example, although there were low levels of interest in programme options at prices above £5 a month, in the light of consumer expenditure on video and Pay TV in the experiments the projections are actually based on a price of £10 a month and project a reasonable level of take-up.

In research of this type the 'concept' is usually of great importance. Responses were obtained only to options which were limited in range, content, detail and 'finish'. Critics argued that a more realistic presentation of the options would obtain a more favourable response to the proposition of cable.

It is, however, instructive that the levels of interest established in the CIT consumer research were very similar to the levels of interest established both in BBC's own research and also in other research which included a very realistic and well-executed presentation of the options. It almost seems that, irrespective of the details of the proposition, people are either for or against subscribing to cable. This places a limit on the maximum uptake.

It is easy to confuse respondents with strange ideas. At no stage in the interview was 'cable' mentioned. The questionnaire focussed on <u>programmes</u>, and on a wider and/or different range of programmes, a concept that is readily understood - particularly with the imminent introduction of Channel 4 and Breakfast TV. The responses, therefore, apply equally to satellite as to cable options, and indeed, to any additional programming on broadcast television.

Indirect Measures of Likely Uptake

The CIT report estimates that TV and radio plus other leisure activities total around 72 hours a week on average, with watching TV accounting for 29% of these activities. This total includes activities carried out simultaneously and will therefore overstate leisure activities. However, compared with the rest of Europe, people in the UK spend a lot of time on leisure pursuits and their leisure activities are very home-based. The Henley Centre is forecasting that leisure will become even more home-based over the next decade (2).

What evidence is there of demand for additional programming? There is the familiar evidence of dissatisfaction in UK with existing TV output. In particular:

89% said there were too many repeats

75% said they often wished there was more choice

58% said they wished there were more channels

48% said they didn't enjoy TV as much as they used to

As far as <u>choice</u> of programmes is concerned, while 42% were satisfied, 41% were dissatisfied; satisfaction is greater with the <u>quality</u> of programmes - 43% satisfied but fewer - 32% were dissatisfied. These levels of dissatisfaction, higher than in the rest of Europe, are reflected in the claim by three in ten to have switched off today or yesterday because there was nothing they wanted to watch.

Feature films emerged as the most popular category of TV output, closely followed by national news. Documentaries, science/wildlife programmes, comedies and sport are each liked by around one in two of the population or more and disliked by 12% or less - except for sport, which is disliked by 28%. The popularity of different types of output is shown below:

---

(2)   Henley Centre: Leisure Futures (Quarterly)

Table 1: % of adults who like/dislike categories of TV programmes

	Liked	Disliked	Like-dislike
	%	%	
Feature Films	66	6	+60
National News	63	5	+58
Documentaries	57	12	+45
Science/wildlife etc.	52	9	+43
Comedies	49	12	+37
Sport	48	28	+20
Serious discussions	27	22	+ 5
Chat shows	26	26	-
Pop rock	24	37	-13
Classical music	19	31	-12
Religion	15	37	-22

Going to any type of cultural activity or spectator sport is very much a minority pastime, but there are significant numbers who would like to go more often:

Table 2: % of adults who ...

to ...	Go once a month or more	Would like to go more often
	%	%
Theatre/opera	3	29
Cinema	7	23
Sport (excluding horse racing)	13	12
Cultural exhibitions	4	12
Pop/rock concerts	2	10

CIT's research would therefore seem to indicate the potential of a TV service offering films or plays/operas in particular but also pop/rock concerts, 'cultural' programmes and sport.

Direct Measures of Likely Uptake

Reactions were established to three different options:

a) One subscription channel - a mixture of recent films and sport. At £5 a month, 26% were interested; half were not at all interested. At £8 a month, only 11% were still interested.

b) A multi-channel service with some special interest and some mixed entertainment programmes; 34% were interested in the idea at no cost; at £5 a month, 27% expressed interest; at £8 a month, only 5% were interested.

c) Single programme-type services: these attracted varied levels of interest, depending on the type of programme:

Table 5: % of Radio Highland Listeners:
Claimed Frequency of Listening to Radio Highland English Programmes (Highland)

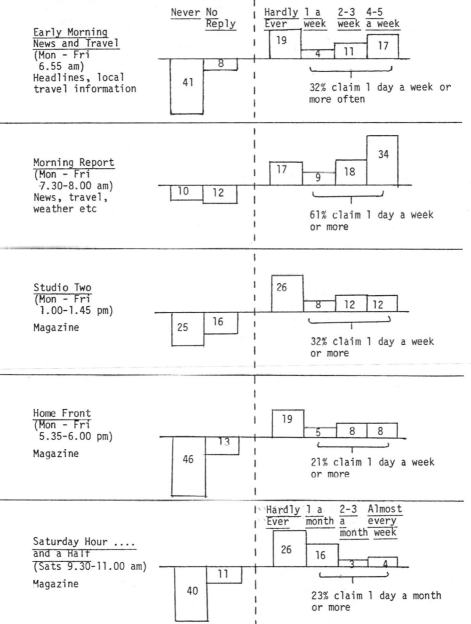

Early Morning
News and Travel
(Mon – Fri
6.55 am)
Headlines, local
travel information

Never: 41   No Reply: 8

Hardly Ever: 19   1 a week: 4   2-3 week: 11   4-5 a week: 17

32% claim 1 day a week or more often

Morning Report
(Mon – Fri
7.30-8.00 am)
News, travel,
weather etc

Never: 10   No Reply: 12

Hardly Ever: 17   1 a week: 9   2-3 week: 18   4-5 a week: 34

61% claim 1 day a week or more

Studio Two
(Mon – Fri
1.00-1.45 pm)
Magazine

Never: 25   No Reply: 16

Hardly Ever: 26   1 a week: 8   2-3 week: 12   4-5 a week: 12

32% claim 1 day a week or more

Home Front
(Mon – Fri
5.35-6.00 pm)
Magazine

Never: 46   No Reply: 13

Hardly Ever: 19   1 a week: 5   2-3 week: 8   4-5 a week: 8

21% claim 1 day a week or more

Saturday Hour ....
and a Half
(Sats 9.30-11.00 am)
Magazine

Never: 40   No Reply: 11

Hardly Ever: 26   1 a month: 16   2-3 a month: 3   Almost every week: 4

23% claim 1 day a month or more

From this limited data, some tentative conclusions can be attempted. Overall, three quarters of those saying they could receive Radio Scotland also said they could receive Radio Highland; this implies that these are VHF listeners. For the remaining quarter, the most likely explanations are that they are either MF listeners, VHF (non-opt-out) listeners or simply unaware of Radio Highland's existence within Radio Scotland's output. These proportions differ between East and West, with the large majority (nine in ten) of Radio Scotland listeners in western areas apparently tuned to VHF opt-out services or tuning between available Radio Scotland versions. In contrast, one in three in the East who say they receive Radio Scotland say they do not receive Radio Highland. Taken with the lower level of VHF set use for these areas this suggests that MF Radio Scotland is more widely known/used in the eastern portion of the Radio Highland area.

In the case of Radio nan Eilean, similar problems do not seem to occur, with a high level of claimed reception and listening being found among those living in its transmission area.

Radio Highland and Radio nan Eilean programmes

Radio Highland produces both English language and Gaelic language programmes. Radio Highland listeners were asked to say how often, if at all they listened to each of service's regular output. (Radio Highland also produces programmes for Radio Scotland's Gaelic service; these have not been included, as the main aim of the research was to examine Radio Highland programmes made for, and broadcast to, the Highlands and Islands). Replies are shown in Table 5. Also included were Radio nan Eilean's main weekly programmes, made largely in Gaelic.

Radio Highland English Programmes

Claimed frequency of listening to specific Radio Highland programmes varies according to the programme. 'Morning Report' is most widely heard, with one in three Radio Highland listeners (one in six of the adult population) claiming to hear it four or five days a week. The profile of those claiming to listen four or five days a week to the various programmes suggests that, on the whole, frequent listeners tend to be aged over 39, female, and to live in the west. 'Morning Report', in particular, has a noticeably large number of ABC1 (upper and middle class) frequent listeners.

Table 6: Claimed Frequency of hearing Radio Highland and Radio nan Eilean Gaelic programmes

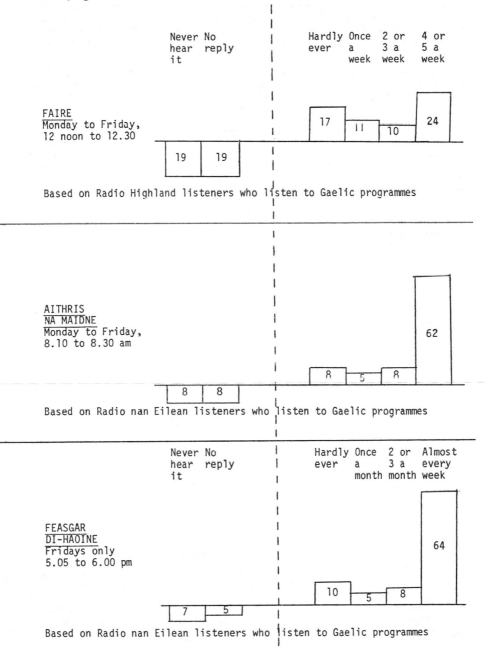

Never hear it   No reply   Hardly ever   Once a week   2 or 3 a week   4 or 5 a week

FAIRE
Monday to Friday,
12 noon to 12.30

19   19   17   11   10   24

Based on Radio Highland listeners who listen to Gaelic programmes

AITHRIS
NA MAIDNE
Monday to Friday,
8.10 to 8.30 am

8   8   8   5   8   62

Based on Radio nan Eilean listeners who listen to Gaelic programmes

Never hear it   No reply   Hardly ever   Once a month   2 or 3 a month   Almost every week

FEASGAR
DI-HAOINE
Fridays only
5.05 to 6.00 pm

7   5   10   5   8   64

Based on Radio nan Eilean listeners who listen to Gaelic programmes

Radio Highland and Radio nan Eilean Gaelic programmes

Each of these Gaelic programmes is widely heard. Listening to these programmes ('Faire', 'Aithris na Maidne', 'Feasgar di-Haoine') is, by and large, the province of Gaelic speakers, most of whom live in the western areas. Among those who do listen, frequent listening (four or five days a week; almost every week for 'Feasgar') is high, suggesting a large and loyal audience among Gaelic speakers living in the West. The most striking findings are for Radio nan Eilean's 'Feasgar di-Haoine' (weekly) and 'Aithris na Maidne' (daily) - over six in ten listeners to the service said they listened frequently. (This represents around half of the adult population). These frequent listeners to Radio nan Eilean Gaelic broadcasts are representative of the population as a whole; listening to Gaelic is not the prerogative of any particular age, sex or social class grouping.

Among the small number of Gaelic-speaking Radio Highland listeners in the Inverness/Moray, Northeast and Argyll/Lochaber area only very few said they listened to 'Faire' as often as four or five days a week. Possibly listening to Gaelic broadcasts is only undertaken or seen as worthwhile in a Gaelic environment, such as the western areas, where large proportions of Gaelic-speaking Radio Highland listeners claimed the same frequency of listening.

General opinions about Radio Highland and Radio nan Eilean

Radio Highland

An indication of listeners' overall attitudes towards Radio Highland was obtained by asking them whether they thought the number of Radio Highland programmes was too few, too many, or about right.

Table 7:

	Radio Highland listeners
	%
Number of Radio Highlands programme is:	
TOO FEW	28
ABOUT RIGHT	62
TOO MANY	*
NO REPLY	10

* = less than 1%

While around threequarters of Radio Highland listeners opted for the neutral 'about right' category (which includes around 10% who did not reply), the remainder almost unanimously opted for 'too few', suggesting a positive attitude in favour of Radio Highland. Overall, though, the predominant impression gained from these results is one of a certain neutrality towards Radio Highland among those claiming to listen to the service, inasmuch as the majority do not want more programmes. If those listening to Radio Highland were highly enthusiastic, a bigger 'too few' proportion would be expected.

Radio nan Eilean

Listeners to Radio nan Eilean were also asked to give their opinions of the number of programmes on this service.

Table 8:	Radio nan Eilean listeners
	%

Number of Radio
nan Eilean programme is:

TOO FEW	51
ABOUT RIGHT	47
TOO MANY	2

In this case, half of those saying they usually listened to Radio nan Eilean said the number of programmes was 'too few', just under half said 'about right' (including 9% who failed to reply) and a tiny number said 'too many'. Compared to Radio Highland, nan Eilean appears to have a more enthusiastic listenership, who want more programmes.

Attitudes to Gaelic radio broadcasting in general

Listening to Gaelic programmes

Small but significant numbers of radio programmes in Scotland are in Gaelic - both on Radio Highland and Radio nan Eilean (around $2\frac{1}{2}$ hours per week) on a regional basis, and on Radio Scotland (around $6\frac{1}{2}$ hours per week) on a national basis. One aim of the research was to examine attitudes to Gaelic language programmes in general among the population of Radio Highland and Radio nan Eilean transmission area. These areas contain the bulk of the total Gaelic-speaking population, albeit as an overall minority in comparison to non-Gaelic speakers living there.

In the population sampled English-only speakers outnumbered Gaelic speakers by four to one. There is therefore a limited audience for fully-understood Gaelic material.

Table 9: Do you ever listen to programmes in Gaelic on the radio these days?

	All Radio listeners	Non-Gaelic speakers	Gaelic speakers
	%	%	%
Yes, ... as many as I can	14	1	63
Yes, ... a few	5	2	16
Yes, ... occasionally	6	5	10
Yes, ... hardly ever	5	5	4
No, never/No reply	70	87	6

While the majority of Gaelic speakers said that they listen to as many Gaelic languages broadcasts as they could, a small number (8%) of English speakers also said they listened to them at least occasionally.

Chart 5:
Attitudes to Gaelic
Radio Programmes

Based on all radio listeners

		ALL	GAELIC SPEAKERS	NON-GAELIC SPEAKERS
		%	%	%
I usually turn off or change stations when a Gaelic programme comes on	Agree	46	4	58
	Neither/No reply	25	24	25
	Disagree	29	73	17
I like those programmes which have Gaelic music in them	Agree	45	83	35
	Neither/No reply	33	15	38
	Disagree	21	2	25
Programmes with both languages together would be helpful to me	Agree	36	38	36
	Neither/No reply	33	16	29
	Disagree	31	16	35
I'm not interested in any Gaelic broadcasts, no matter what kind of programme	Agree	36	2	46
	Neither/No reply	28	17	31
	Disagree	36	80	24
There should be a wider range of different kinds of programme in Gaelic	Agree	25	72	13
	Neither/No reply	49	24	55
	Disagree	26	3	30
Most Gaelic radio programmes are on at times which are inconvenient for me	Agree	10	21	7
	Neither/No reply	66	45	72
	Disagree	24	34	21
I prefer to hear programmes in Gaelic rather than in English	Agree	9	45	1
	Neither/No reply	36	46	32
	Disagree	55	9	67
I usually only listen to Gaelic broadcasts	Agree	4	16	1
	Neither/No reply	26	34	24
	Disagree	70	50	75

Specific attitudes to Gaelic radio programming

These results give a broad picture of listening to Gaelic programmes; however, a further series of agree/disagree statements about Gaelic programmes was included so as to disentangle the different reasons, opinions and motivations underlying these overall listening patterns. The proportions of radio listeners agreeing or disagreeing with each statement are shown facing.

The replies from the non-Gaelic speakers leave little doubt that, for large numbers, Gaelic programmes are avoided or uninteresting. However, substantial minorities disagreed that they usually switched off (one in six), or that they were not interested in any Gaelic programmes (one in four). In the specific cases of Gaelic music, and bilingual programmes non-Gaelic speaking listeners are almost equally split between 'agree', 'disagree' and the intermediate, neutral 'neither agree nor disagree' option. Overall, the non-Gaelic speakers show a certain 'live and let live' tendency and do not unanimously endorse the more anti-Gaelic statements.

In a similar vein, many Gaelic-speaking listeners to Gaelic broadcasts disagree with the statement expressing strongly partisan views ('... only listen to Gaelic ...'). Substantial minorities of this group and of the non-Gaelic listeners appear to have similar views on the usefulness of bilingual programmes, representing a possible point of contact between the two cultures (a similar shared area is also found for Gaelic music programmes). However, it is clear that many Gaelic speakers have a strong preference for Gaelic over English, with almost half agreeing that they preferred to hear Gaelic.

Gaelic Television Programmes

While the main aims of the research - and, consequently, the bulk of the questionnaire - were concerned with radio, a few questions on television were included so as to allow a modest examination of opinion and behaviour relating to Gaelic television broadcasting.

Viewing of Gaelic television programmes

Compared to Gaelic provision on radio, there are fewer Gaelic language television programmes, and those that are transmitted (by BBC and ITV) tend to be relegated to late evening slots.

Claimed viewing of Gaelic programmes was as follows.

Table 10: Viewing of Gaelic programmes on TV

	All viewers	Non-Gaelic speaking viewers	Gaelic-speaking viewers
	%	%	%
Watch Gaelic TV nowadays	23	12	70
Do not watch Gaelic TV nowadays	77	88	30

As with listening to Gaelic radio broadcasts, a small number of non-Gaelic speaking viewers claim to watch Gaelic television, together with the majority of Gaelic speakers. Almost one third of the latter, though, said they did not watch Gaelic programmes.

All those saying they did not watch Gaelic programmes were asked why. Replies have been grouped into the broad categories shown below.

Table 11: Non-viewing of Gaelic TV programmes

	Viewers who do not watch Gaelic TV programmes	
	Non-Gaelic speakers	Gaelic speakers
	%	%
Reasons given:		
"Can't understand Gaelic"	57	0
"Not interested in them"	10	9
"On too late at night"	3	47
"Would watch if subtitled"	1	0
"Clashes with other programmes"	1	0
"Poor quality of programmes"	1	5
Other reasons given	4	12
No reason given	28	28

Among non-Gaelic speaking viewers by far the largest (almost six out of ten), and most predictable reason given was the inability to understand Gaelic. The only other reason given by a much smaller proportion (one in ten) was lack of interest.

Gaelic-speakers who did not watch Gaelic TV programmes gave as their most common reason the late timing of these programmes. However, a few (one in ten) also gave lack of interest as their reason, and one in twenty mentioned poor quality.

Attitudes towards Gaelic television programmes

As a broad measure of opinions about Gaelic television, all television viewers were asked to state whether they felt the number of these programmes was too few, about right, or too many.

Table 12: Opinions of number of Gaelic TV programmes

Number of Gaelic
TV programme is:

	All viewers	Non-Gaelic speaking viewers	Gaelic-speaking viewers
	%	%	%
TOO FEW	24	12	69
ABOUT RIGHT/ NO REPLY	65	75	29
TOO MANY	11	13	1

A majority of all viewers (over six in ten) felt that the number of television programmes in Gaelic was 'about right' or did not offer their opinion. The proportion saying 'too few' is over twice as large as that saying 'too many'. Overall, the balance of opinion among television viewers as whole is that the number is about right: Among non-Gaelic speaking viewers, this also holds, but the majority of the Gaelic speaking viewers differ sharply, and want more programmes.

Table 13:	Very Interested	Fairly Interested	Not very Interested	Not at all Interested /No reply	% Balance:*
Inverness and Moray	63	22	5	9	+71
Aberdeen	25	32	16	27	+14
Western Isles	26	29	19	25	+11
Glasgow and Edinburgh	17	38	19	25	+11
Wester Ross	16	31	21	31	- 5
Oban and the Argyll Islands	13	25	27	36	-25
Caithness area	12	28	26	34	-20
Lochaber area	11	27	26	35	-23
Orkney and Shetland	8	29	28	36	-27

* % balance is calculated by: % very or fairly interested
                                  - % not very or not at all
                                      interested/no reply

a + value means an overall balance interested in an area.

a - value means an overall balance not interested in it.

Interest in local and regional news and information

A subsidiary aim of the research was to establish the degree of interest among people living in the Highlands and Islands in news and information about various parts of Scotland. All respondents were asked to state how interested they were in hearing news and information from each of a variety of locations in the Highlands and Islands, and in other areas of Scotland.

Table 13 shows interest in each area, and interested/not interested balance among the total sample. (In this, missing replies have been assumed to mean 'not at all interested').

Of all the areas, only Inverness and Moray is regarded as being of interest by a large majority of the sample. With the other areas, it is clear that there are substantial differences of opinion within the sample, with large numbers being in direct disagreement (for example, the Western Isles, where the numbers say 'very interested' and 'not at all interested' are equal). From these results, it is reasonable to suppose that news about any one area is going to receive a mixed welcome among the Highlands and Islands population as a whole. This is especially important for a service such as Radio Highland.

This overall picture conceals a further, obvious factor; the relation between where people live and where they are interested in hearing about. The table below shows overall balance of interest in different places among those living in different sampling areas.

Table 14:   % balance among those living in:

Interested in:

	Inverness/ Moray	North East	Argyll/ Lochaber	Skye/ West Coast	Lewis	Uists
Inverness & Moray	+88	+88	-10	+42	+30	+18
Aberdeen	+26	+16	-26	-12	- 6	-46
Western Isles	-10	- 6	+22	+62	+88	+94
Glasgow & Edinburgh	+ 2	+12	+ 6	+20	+38	+66
Wester Ross	-18	+34	-38	+34	- 2	-32
Oban & Argyll Islands	-38	-38	+64	-20	-20	+44
Caithness area	-20	+10	-56	-34	-42	+38
Lochaber area	-26	-36	+30	-20	-36	- 6
Orkney & Shetland	-28	-16	-42	-24	-24	-28
(Base)	(415)	(144)	(49)	(180)	(327)	(88)

Key: a + value means that more people are interested in that particular area than are not interested.

a - value means that more people are not interested in that particular area than are interested.

These figures represent the overall balance of views in each area, the majority view. In all areas there are minorities who differ from the majority. Several features of differing interest levels are shown.

(1) People living in the East (Inverness, Moray, and the eastern parts of Ross and Cromarty and Sutherland) are largely interested in their own areas and Aberdeen, and not interested in other areas of the Highlands and Islands. There is a certain degree of overall interest in Central Scotland (Glasgow and Edinburgh), but this is far lower than that shown in Aberdeen.

(2) People living in the West (Skye, western parts of Ross and Cromarty and Sutherland, the Western Isles) on the other hand are united by an overall lack of interest in Aberdeen and an interest in Glasgow and Edinburgh. Also, they all tend to share interests in their own or immediately neighbouring area.

(3) Transport, rather than simple geography, appears to influence interest. Those living in the Uists (including Benbecula and Barra) express interest in Oban, the Argyll Islands - corresponding to the main transport routes out of Oban (and, ultimately, Glasgow rather than Inverness). In contrast, those living on Lewis and Harris overall are not interested in Oban, but show a higher interest in Inverness.

(4) All areas - with the solitary exception of the small sample from Argyll and Lochaber - are united in overall interest in Inverness and Moray and disinterest in the Orkneys and Shetlands.

(5) While the Argyll/Lochaber group is very small and therefore of limited validity, it does seem likely that they represent a different set of interests from any of the other areas. No other groups expressed any overall interest in Lochaber, or (apart from these living on the Uists) in Oban and the associated Islands.

Overall, these figures show a potential problem for any news service based on such a wide region; news for any one area within the region could, potentially at least, alienate listeners in another. Obviously, though, this will depend largely on the nature of news and information coverage and its relevance outside its immediate source. There are, however, common strands which unite all areas except Lochaber and Argyll.

7. THE EFFECTIVENESS OF A
TV SERIES DESIGNED TO
HELP SMOKERS TO GIVE UP

Nadine Dyer, Manager (Special Projects)

1. ### Introduction

The six part BBC series "So You Want to Stop Smoking" was the subject of an extensive evaluation programme sponsored by the BBC, the Health Education Council, the Scottish Health Education Group, and the DHSS in Northern Ireland.

The aim of the evaluation was to assess the effects of, and reactions to, the series and its backup literature, both of which were designed to help smokers who wanted to give up to do so. There were five separate elements to the evaluation:-

Audience size and composition

i.   The 'climate of opinion' about smoking among the general public, measured twice before and once after the series.

ii.   Reactions to individual programmes and to the series as a whole, involving the examination of detailed responses to each aspect of the programmes.

iii. The (claimed and apparent) effectiveness of the series in helping smokers to give up.

iv.   Reactions to the booklet contained in the backup literature pack.

This paper will deal mainly with item (iii), the claimed and apparent effectiveness of the series. Some information about audience size and composition, and about the series and the booklet will be provided to place the study of "effectiveness" in context.

2. ### The series and the back-up literature

The series was shown on six successive Sundays from Jan. 3rd 1982 at 5.45pm, and repeated on Tuesdays from 5th Jan. at 3.45pm.

Each episode, introduced by a well-known and popular presenter of medical programmes, followed the progress of four smokers who were trying to give up. All were in clerical or manual occupations and had smoked heavily for several years. Two were married women with non-smoking husbands; the other two were a couple who were both trying to give up. They were interviewed each week about the advantages and difficulties of giving up smoking. Advice from a chest specialist was also featured throughout while a diet expert was a guest in one episode.

The series followed a plan, echoed in the booklet, progressing from planning and preparing to stop smoking, through stopping to planning to remain a non-smoker. After each episode, viewers were invited to write in for a free "Stop Pack" which contained a booklet entitled "So You Want to Stop Smoking", a letter from the presenter and a contract for the intending stopper to sign.

3. Audience size and composition

3.1. Size and share

Audience size and composition were measured using the routine system employed for every programme by the BBC and Independent Television.*

Table 1:   Sundays - 5.45pm

1982	%	millions
Jan 3rd	16.2	8.3
Jan 10th	15.6	8.0
Jan 17th	15.4	7.9
Jan 24th	15.6	8.0
Jan 31st	15.0	7.7
Feb 7th	14.1	7.2

Source: Television Audiences: BBC Reports issued by BARB (1)

The size of the audience was fairly typical for a programme on a winter Sunday evening on BBC1, with around 8 million people watching each episode of "So You Want to Stop Smoking". The audience was somewhat larger for the first episode, which was broadcast during the first week of January - a holiday period for many.

Audiences appear to drop slightly towards the end of the series. However, the television audience for all three channels dropped slightly during these weeks. Throughout, a quarter of all viewers were tuned to SYWTSS.

3.2 "Loyalty" and composition

Data obtained from the routine measurement system was re-analysed to show firstly, the extent to which people who watched one episode watched others, and secondly, who, in demographic terms, was watching.

Half of the population aged 16+ saw any of the series at all: a fifth saw one episode and only 2% saw all six. This pattern is fairly typical for a popular BBC1 series.

The audience composition, too, was typical for this slot. By and large, it was a good reflection of the population, although it had a slight bias towards older people, women and the middle classes.

---

(1) Described in 'Continuous Research for Television and Radio: The 1980's approach' in Annual Review of BBC Broadcasting Research Findings No.8, ch.1.

4. Apparent and claimed effectiveness of the series

4.1. Aim

The aim of this element of the evaluation was to assess the extent to which

a)   smokers who watched the series gave up, and

b)   smokers who watched the series and gave up claimed the series had influenced them.

4.2   Method

At an early stage in planning the research, it was estimated that, if a random sample of the population were used, a very large sample size would be needed to detect changes in behaviour among smokers. It was therefore decided to restrict this survey to people who said in November 1981, that they smoked cigarettes.

Interviewers working on the BBC's Daily Survey (2) were instructed to ask all adult respondents whether or not they smoked cigarettes. For each smoker, the number smoked per day and the smoker's name and address were recorded. This procedure continued for 9 days in England and Wales. In order to accumulate sufficient numbers to produce separate results for Scotland and N.Ireland, the collection of smokers' names and addresses continued for 15 days in Scotland and 19 days in N. Ireland. In all, 4429 smokers were contacted. In March 1982, after the end of the series, a postal questionnaire about current smoking behaviour, viewing of the series, methods used to try to give up and so on, was sent to all 4429 smokers.

4.3   The sample

Two-thirds of those contacted returned usable questionnaires - an average response for this type of postal survey. The 2,619 replies were matched up with the original sample of contacted smokers and weights were applied to compensate for the initial oversampling in Scotland and N. Ireland. Despite the fact that one third of those contacted did not reply, (3) the final sample compared very well in demographic terms to both the UK population and the smokers contacted in November.

Respondents were also compared, in terms of their smoking behaviour, both with the November sample and with data from another stage of the evaluation.

---

(2)   The Daily Survey in November '81 was the BBC's tool for continuous measurement of Radio Audence size. It is a quota sample (N = 2000 per day) within a stratified random selection of local authority areas, and is designed to be representative of the UK population aged 4+.

(3)   It should be borne in mind when looking at the results that two-fifths of the sample did not respond. It has to be assumed that none of the non-respondents gave up smoking, in order to examine the findings according to the most stringent criteria when extrapolating to the population.

Table 2: Demographics

		UK % (Base) (pop)	Smokers** in November (3,602)	Respondents** to postal % (1,947)
SEX:	Men	49*	52	52
	Women	51	46	48
	n.a.		2	
AGE:	16-19	9*	8	9
	20-29	18	21	22
	30-49	32	34	35
	50-64	22	25	24
	65+	19	11	10
REGION:	England	83*	81	81
	Wales	5	6	6
	N.I.	3	3	2
	Scotland	9	11	11
CLASS:***	A)) B)	30	23	25
	Cx	40	40	39
	Cy	30	35	34
	n.a.		2	2
EMPLOYMENT STATUS:	Employed	54+	59	60
	Student	3	3	3
	Not employed	43	38	37

*   Source: OPCS mid 1980 estimates
**   All figures based on weighted data
***   BBC BRD definition
+   Source: Department of Employment figures.

Table 3: Smoking Behaviour

	November sample (all) 3602 %	March respondents (all) 1947 %	"Climate of opinion" Dec 1981 (all) 1852 %
Smoking	100	87	38
Not smoking	0	13	62

	cigarette smokers 3602 %	cigarette smokers 1693 %	cigarette smokers 651 %
10 or less	34	24	35
11-20	45	49	46
21-30	11	18	10
31 or more	7	5	6
handroll	4	3	3
n.a.	-	1	-

When smoking behaviour from November to March is compared, it is at once evident that a sizeable minority - 13% - gave up between November and March. Of those who gave up, just under half did so before the series and just over half, during or after it. Other studies (4) of smoking have found similarly that there is considerable movement between respondents defined as smokers and those defined as ex-smokers when questioned at different times. When cigarette smokers are compared, while the November sample closely resembles the "Climate of Opinion" sample, the March respondents who were still smoking present a very different picture. Many fewer of them were light smokers, and more of them were heavier smokers.

---

(4) Of 1,281 smokers recontacted six months after an interview about smoking, 453 (35%) had made at least one attempt to give up since the interview. (Smoking Attitudes and Behaviour: Alan Marsh and Jil Mattheson, OPCS, 1983).

4.4   Giving up and cutting down (March)

Table 4:

	All (base = 1947) %	Viewers (856) %	Non-viewers (1039) (n.a. = 52) %
Given up			
November - 3rd January	6	6	6
3rd-31st January	4	6	2
31st January-March	3	4	3
Cut down			
November-3rd January	12	12	13
3rd-31st January	8	11	5
31st January-March	5	5	5
Smoking same as or more than in November '81			
Same	57	52	61
More	4	4	4
Other/n.a.	2	0	1

When viewers and non-viewers are compared, rates of giving up before the series were the same across the whole sample. During the series, the rate of giving up was twice as high among viewers as among non-viewers. Although the overall numbers involved are perhaps small - 52 smokers watched the series and gave up when it was on - this finding is highly statistically significant.

Table 5:

Smokers at 3rd January	Viewers (805)	Non-viewers (981)
Gave up 3rd-31st	52	26
Did not give up 3rd 31st	753	955

(X^2 = 15.356 p < 0.001 at 1 degree of freedom)

Similarly, viewers were much more likely than non-viewers to have cut down. Nearly a third of the respondents who were smoking at the 3rd January and who subsequently watched the series had modified their smoking behaviour by March.

Table 6:   **Modification in smoking behaviour and watching the series**

| | Smokers at 3rd Jan | |
	Viewers (805) %	Non-viewers (981) %
gave up/cut down during or after series	28	17
cut down before 3rd	12	13
Smoking same/more/other	60	70

Clearly, then, there is a relationship between having seen the series at all, and moderating smoking behaviour. There was also a marked relationship between the number of episodes seen and modification in smoking behaviour.

Table 7:   **Smoking behaviour and amount of series seen**

No. of episodes seen	all* sample (1947) %	gave up during or after series (142) %	cut down during or after series (245) %	smoking same or more (1148) %	gave up before series (109) %
Seen any at all	44	61	56	41	47
None	53	39	44	59	53
1-2	33	34	38	33	38
3-4	9	19	14	6	6
5-6	2	8	4	2	3

While slightly smaller proportions of this sample of smokers and ex-smokers than of the population as a whole saw any of the series - 44%, as compared to 50%, it was immediately apparent that more of those who gave up than of those who were continuing to smoke saw the series. Not only did more of the givers up and cutters down watch at all, they were also more likely to watch more episodes. This is especially marked in the case of those who gave up. Just over 1 in 10 of the whole sample watched 3 or more episodes, whereas nearly 3 in 10 of the givers up did so.

---

* Non-response to amount of series seen = 52 (3% of total) excluded from this and subsequent tables.

4.5. Possible other effects

It has been shown above that viewers were more likely than non-viewers to give up, and conversely that not only were givers up more likely to watch than continuing smokers, they were also more likely to watch more episodes. The question arises next as to whether any other variables could be operating to cause certain groups of smokers a) to watch more readily b) to give up more readily c) both. In this context, both demographic variables and previous cigarette consumption were examined. Virtually no differences in demographic profile were found between viewers and non-viewers. Similarly, the demographic profiles of those who were moderating their smoking behaviour and those who were not, whether or not they watched the series, were very similar.

Table 8:

		all sample*		gave up/cut down at		smoking same or more + other	
		saw series	did not see	saw series	did not see	saw series	did not see
		(856)	(1039)	(380)	(370)	(470)	(675)
AGE	16-19	10	8	10	10	10	7
	20-29	23	21	22	21	25	21
	30-49	35	35	36	32	35	35
	50-64	23	25	23	27	23	25
	65+	8	10	10	9	6	11
	n.a.	-	1	-	-	1	1
SEX	male	50	54	48	53	51	53
	female	49	46	51	45	47	45
	n.a.	1	0	1	1	2	2
CLASS	A	5	4	5	4	6	4
	B	20	21	21	19	20	21
	Cx	40	39	41	42	40	38
	Cy	33	34	33	33	33	34
	n.a.	2	2	1	2	2	2

*non response to whether saw series excluded.

114

4.6   The claimed effect of the series

Of the sample of 1947, 110 gave up before the series began: the subsequent analysis will be based only on those who were smoking at the beginning of the series.

Table 9: Smoking behaviour

All in sample	1837	of which SAW SYWTSS		806	
gave up during or after series	144	"	"	86	) NB:) raw figures) not percentages
cut down during or after	745	"	"	137	

86 out of the 806 smokers who watched the series (11%) gave up smoking during or after the series. Of these 86 smokers, 10 claimed the series was wholly responsible for their giving up, and 36 that it was partly responsible.

Smokers who saw SYWTSS	806
	(%)
saw SYWTSS and gave up	11
series at all responsible for giving up	6

Thus, 6% of smokers who watched the series claimed it had been at all influential in their decision to give up. Among those who watched and gave up, over half attributed the giving up at least partly to the series. Of course, it should be borne in mind that members of the sample who did not reply - over a third of the sample - may have had very different behaviour patterns from respondents. Even if the inclusion of non-respondents effectively decreased the proportion of those in the sample who claimed the series had influenced them to give up by half, at 3% of all smoker-viewers, this would not be a negligible result.

4.7   Extrapolating to the population

One of the aims of the evaluation was to assess whether, and to what the extent, the series may have lead smokers to give up or cut down.   Clearly, the data must be treated according to the most stringent criteria. It must therefore be assumed that among the original sample of 3,602, no non-respondents gave up or cut down having watched the series.

Table 10:

Total sample =	3602
(Estimate)* gave up before series (6%) =	216
Smokers at 3rd Jan =	3386
(Estimate)* viewers among sample (44%) =	1584
Smoker viewers: Gave up during/after =	86 (= 5.4%+ 1.67)**
Smoker viewers who gave up during/after and said series influential =	46 (= 2.9%+ 1.24)**
Smoker viewers: Cut down during/after =	137 (= 8.6% + 2.07)**
Smoker viewers who cut down during/after who said series influential =	80 (= 5.05% + 0.88)**

<u>Population Estimates</u>

Adult population (16+) =	43,169,700
Viewers = 50%*** =	21,584,800
Smoker-viewers = 38% of audience =	8,202,200

<u>GIVING UP</u>

At the 95% confidence level, it can be assumed that 5.4% (+ 1.67) of smoker-viewers gave up during or after the series:- that is between 303,000 and 514,000 smokers. Of them, between 139,000 and 336,000 would say the series influenced them to give up.

<u>CUTTING DOWN</u>

At the 95% confidence level, it can be estimated that 8.6% (+ 2.07) of smoker-viewers cut down during or after the series:- that is between 535,000 and 875,000. Of these between 342,000 and 486,000 would say the series had influenced them to do so.

---

*   Estimates taken from findings based on respondents.

**   SE at 95% confidence level, DEFF estimated at 1.5

***   BARB estimates.

OVERALL

Around half a million smoker-viewers are likely to have given up, having watched the series, and slightly over half of them would say the series had influenced their giving up. Taking givers up and cutters down together, at the minimum estimate, one smoker in ten has moderated or given up smoking after having seen some of the series. Over half of these smokers and ex-smokers are likely to say the series played some part in influencing their decision to give up or cut down.

8. Q.E.D.: RESEARCH FOR A SECOND SERIES

Anne Laking, Researcher (Special Projects)

Mick Rhodes, Executive Producer (Science and Features)

Introduction

The relationship between media practitioners and researchers has been the subject of much recent debate (1) - the current consensus cynically asserts that no fruitful relationship can exist. "Practitioners", it is said, "criticise the language and limitations of much research dogma and their expectations of research are often too high. Researchers, on the other hand, commonly fail to understand the practical problems of media production" (2). Happily, however, it is our experience that not only is fruitful and effective co-operation between researchers and producers possible, but that it is the rule rather than the exception. The research reported here is one example of such collaboration, where the evaluation of the first of the new Q.E.D. series played an important part in the development of further Q.E.D. series.

The paper describes the development of Q.E.D. generally but emphasises the way the Executive Producer used BRD's services in making production decisions. Anne Laking of BRD outlines the research aims, design, and results; Mick Rhodes the Executive Producer, describes the impact of the research from a production point of view. Mick Rhodes starts the story.

The Media Practitioners Problem

The problem was simple to describe. It was August 1981 and the task was to get going a new BBC-1 science series to occupy the middle ground between the usually optimistic, five-minute items of "Tomorrow's World" and the fifty-minute, often heavy-duty "Horizon". Of course the snag was that it had to hold its own in the audience-catching battles of the BBC-1 schedules. "Tomorrow"s World" often drew audiences of above 10 million.

Horizon, on BBC-2, was happy with $3\frac{1}{2}$ million. It seemed to me that the new series would need to average about 8 million if it was to keep the ££'s rolling out of controller BBC-1's purse. This figure I voiced around - and everybody laughed.

At this stage I made some basic, very basic, decisions. I assumed that we were trying to produce a series that could run for ever. So it must never run out of subjects. It followed that its brief had to be wide, whereas its predecessors, "Open Secret" and "The Risk Business" had quite specific and narrow aims. And I assumed that our audience would be essentially scientifically illiterate and that all science was new to them. The aim of the series was not to sit uncomfortably on the sharp cutting edge of science. And, anyway, Horizon already did that well, while "Tomorrow's World" dealt promptly

---

(1)   Discussion from "Representation in the Mass Media" Conference, April 1983.

(2)   Jon Baggaley et al "Psychology of the T.V. Image" (Praeger, 1980).

and efficiently with technical innovations. No, our 'patch' was the vast body of science, medicine and technology that was fascinating and fun but no longer in the pages of New Scientist. In my mind I visualised this area as somehow resembling the Science Museum - and especially the basement where all those kids - and grown-up kids - seem to have so much fun playing with assorted machines and discovering things that everybody else knew anyway!

A final assumption was not an assumption but a personal edict: that our programmes must be centrally based in science or medicine or technology. We wouldn't bend subjects that were generally interesting but devoid of science so that they would "fit" - the science was not going to be spread like Marmite on unscientific bread.

So that's where we were by the end of September 1981. Producers were in their offices; work was starting; and everybody was asking "what's the brief?". To which I simply replied "8 million - and centrally based in science" for I deliberately wanted to encourage as many solutions to the problem as possible. That way we would see which solutions worked and there would be variety for me to exercise good evolutionary selection pressures on. Then we could evolve. If I laid down more detailed rules I'd perhaps have fewer mistakes but certainly less variety - and we'd learn less.

It was at about this point that Broadcasting Research Department came into it. My first use of audience research was simply to survey all the past Science and Features Department output to see what programmes in the past had attracted 8 million viewers. The answer was clear ... there was Tomorrow's World ... and Tomorrow's World ... but the Burke Specials had reached an average of 10 million for two series. And that was it ...

Table 1.

Average Audience for science programmes since 1977

Connections - James Burke	1978 Oct/Dec	6.7 million
The Real Thing - James Burke	1980 Mar/Apr	6.3 "
The Risk Business	1978 June/Aug	3.3 "
	1979 Feb/Mar	4.2 "
	1980 Apr/May	4.0 "
	1981 Apr/May	4.6 "
Open Secret	1980 Feb/Apr	3.8 "
	1981 Jan/Mar	2.5 "
The Secret War	1977 Jan/Feb	7.6 "
Burke Specials	1972 Jun/Jul	5.7 "
	1973 Mar/Apr	10.0 "
	1973 Jun/Jul	6.4 "
	1974 Mar/Apr	6.1 "
	1976 Apr/May	10.1 "
Tomorrow's World	1978 Jan/Dec	7.7 "
	1979 Jan/Dec	8.8 "
	1980 Jan/Dec	8.0 "
	1981 Jan/Jul	8.2 "
	1981 Aug/Dec*	8.7 "

The variation between the various Burke Special series seemed interesting and so I asked Audience Research Department for an analysis. The answer, convincingly argued, came back that the variation was almost totally dependent on the strength of what ITV was offering.

---

*   The new BARB system came in at this point.

The general lack of audiences of 8 millions or so was not good news, but in an earlier life I'd invented Wildlife on One which now frequently picks up audiences of 12 million or more with an occasional 14 million, when its predecessors on BBC-1 - Cousteaus and the like - seldom achieved 8 million. I tried to convince myself that if it could be done once, then why not twice? Hope was, perforce, in the ascendancy.

Now somewhat nervous, I asked BRD to check general preferences for a partly notional set of 10 programmes with two line descriptions of the kind the Evening Standard might carry. These questions were asked on the BRD's Omnibus survey in March 1982.

The ten basic programme descriptions were as follows:-

THE PROOF OF THE PUDDING

How to make tough meat tender, and why souffles collapse and sauces thicken. Cooking as chemistry.

CONSUMERS' GUIDE TO ARMAGEDDON

What a one megaton bomb would do to London. Two couples try out fall-out shelters for ten days.

RIDING ON AIR

Birds and planes and how they fly by the same rules.

GIZMO

A catalogue of man's maddest inventions. Rocket-powered roller skates and kite-powered cars.

HOW TO PICK UP GIRLS, WIN ARGUMENTS AND INFLUENCE PEOPLE

Everybody's guide to the unwritten rules - of dress, conversation, body language, office layout and oratory - and winning.

THE HEART OF THE MATTER

After heart transplants come mechanical hearts - by the year 2000, they could be widely used.

THE VIEW FROM SPACE

What the satellites can really see - and who's using the information.

THE FINAL TEST

The shroud of Turin bears the image of a crucified man. Is it a fake or the true burial cloth of Christ?

MUSIC, MUSIC, MUSIC

What it is and why some tunes make us happy and some make us sad.

LIGHT CREATURES OF THE NIGHT

Special photography shows the ingenuity of creatures that talk by going flash in the dark.

A representative sample of 959 adults was interviewed at home. The question posed was:-

"I am going to show you information about some programmes, and for each, I want you to tell me whether you yourself would watch it.
Would you yourself watch it or not?
Is that definitely or probably?"

The results are as tabulated below:-

Table 2:

	Total %	Positive Interest Men %	Women %	Women : Men**
The Heart of the Matter	64	63	64	1.0
Light Creatures*	62	66	60	0.9
Music, Music, Music*	61	59	63	1.1
Riding on Air*	56	68	44	0.6
View from Space (Spy in the Sky)*	55	69	43	0.6
Armageddon*	49	59	39	0.7
The Final Test	49	44	54	1.2
Gizmo	46	61	32	0.5
Proof of the Pudding*	44	26	65	2.5
How to Pick Up Girls*	39	43	36	0.8

---

*   Actually broadcast in series one.

**   A ratio of 1.0 means that women were as likely as men to express a positive interest.

A ratio of 1.5 means that women were one and a half times as likely to express a positive interest.

A ratio of 0.5 means that women were half as likely to express a positive interest.

Etc...

The date is now April 1982 and the first series of programmes - now called "Q.E.D." is due for transmission. As a result of our prospective survey I selected my 7 programmes and placed them in their transmission order. At first I left out "Riding on Air" and included "Music, Music, Music" as a response to our readings of audience preference. Later a change of schedules made me include both.

The first series was transmitted at 7.40 pm on Tuesdays in April and May 1982. In due course the audience data arrived:-

Table 3:

Title	Audience Millions	Share	Appreciation Index (AI)
How to pick up girls ...	5.2	25.5%	n/a
Light Creatures of the Night	4.5	20.0%	79
Proof of the Pudding	4.2	19.4%	78
Spy in the Sky	5.4	27.0%	82
Beyond the Six Second Mile	6.1	27.5%	80
Music, Music, Music	3.7	17.9%	71
Riding on Air	5.5	26.6%	86
Guide to Armageddon	4.2	30.0%	88
Average	4.8	24.2%	81

Well, not exactly 8 million even though the AI's seemed encouragingly high. But only once did we build on the previous BBC-1 audience - and at 7.40 pm we had to do more than that. Nevertheless, everybody was very kind. Indeed we even managed to congratulate each other quite a lot. After all "you have broken the mould" they said - and I still wonder what that really means.

It was now early summer 1982 and a second series of Q.E.D. was approaching fast. Now was the time to exert some of that evolutionary pressure - but before I could do that I needed more knowledge of how the viewers had perceived the series. First, I checked reality against our prospective survey. How, for example, had "Music", and "Riding on Air" done against each other? Prospectively, "Music, Music, Music" had seemed the more popular ...

Music, Music, Music	3.7 million	AI 71
Riding on Air	5.5	86

Clearly the reality did not match the survey - and that may of course be for many reasons. For example the audience for "Music" was heavily battered by a snooker final on BBC-2. And of course one programme may have lived up better to its description than the other.

With the advantage of hindsight it's worth comparing the rank order from the prospective survey with transmission performance for the seven programmes that were actually broadcast.

Table 4:

Title	Survey	Rank Order Audience size	AI
Light Creatures of the Night	1	4	4
Music, Music, Music	2	6	6
Riding on Air	3	1	2
Spy in the Sky	4	2	3
Guide to Armageddon	5	5 Equal	1
Proof of the Pudding	6	5 Equal	5
How to pick up girls	7	3	7

The Omnibus question, one would assume, should relate to audience size rather than AI, in which case the fit is quite good for "Riding on Air", "Spy in the Sky", "Armageddon" and "Proof of the Pudding" with "Light Creatures of the Night", "Music, Music, Music" and "Girls" being well adrift. So at this point, in May 1982, the one decision that I had taken purely on the basis of audience research - to transmit "Music" not "Riding on Air" would have been wrong had it come to pass! However, there was a very positive point that emerged from this survey: that some subjects appealed quite differently across the sexes. But not only across the sexes - also with age. For example, men were much more interested than women in "Riding on Air"; the reverse was true for "Proof of the Pudding" and youngsters went for "How to pick up girls ..."

Retrospectively it is obvious, but it was this survey that started to make me realise how important it was for subjects not to be too uninteresting to any large group of the potential audience.

Interesting though this was, I needed a much wider base of information and so apart from the prospective survey, I asked BRD to glean as much guidance for me from a retrospective project on the series as possible ... Anne Laking designed the project. Her account follows:-

Enter The Researcher

The first series of Q.E.D. was broadcast in April and May 1982, at 7.30pm on Tuesdays on BBC-1 (3). As Mick Rhodes has described, it was a new series which aimed to popularise science and technology, and present a wide range of different subjects.

The target audience was a fairly down-market, mass audience and it was hoped that Q.E.D. would present a wide range of different scientific subjects in ways which would both appeal to and be easily understood by this type of audience. The approach was strictly non-didactic; it was hoped that viewers would learn from the programmes, but in a relatively passive way. The series was the first of (possibly) three Q.E.D. series and it was seen, in part, as experimental in what was regarded as quite a new departure from the rest of the Science and Features output.

---

(3)   The last programme in the series "A consumer's guide to Armageddon", was shown on 26th July, after the research was completed. This paper, therefore, only refers to the first seven programmes in the series.

Research Aims

At a meeting with Mick Rhodes and the producers of the programme the aims of the research were defined as to evaluate audience reaction to the first Q.E.D. series in order to provide results which would be useful as input in developing future series. The need for research was twofold:- firstly, the first series had always been seen as experimental and some feedback on the success or otherwise of the different styles of presentation was essential. Secondly, the production team wanted to attract an audience of 8 million. So research was required to investigate the elements within the series which may have contributed to a lower level of appeal than had been expected.

In more specific terms the aims of the research were to investigate:

-    whether (and how) viewers categorised the series

-    how well viewers understood the programmes

-    their satisfaction with, interest in, and enjoyment of the programmes

-    reactions to the different styles of presentation

-    and whether the programmes were seen as a series

From this, it was hoped that an understanding of the elements in the series which were important to viewers could be built up. These audience values could then be incorporated with established production values (which are often, but not always, the same) in developing the next Q.E.D. series.

Research Design

The information which would be of most use to producers was detailed, in-depth reactions from viewers. It was decided, therefore, to convene six small groups of about 8 Q.E.D. viewers from the general public (recruited by trained interviewers) to discuss science programmes in general and Q.E.D. programmes in particular. At each group one of three (4) of the Q.E.D. programmes was shown about halfway through the session. The discussions were conducted in the relatively informal atmosphere of an interviewer's home. They were allowed to flow fairly freely - group members were encouraged to talk to each other and not to the researcher - though guided by the researcher to clarify obscure points, identify differences of opinion or ensure that areas of interest to the producers were covered. Since the viewers themselves set the agenda for discussion, the areas which were most important to them were highlighted.

The groups were held both in and outside London with male and female viewers (i.e. they had seen at least one of the Q.E.D. programmes) who were largely lower middle or skilled working class. None of the group members was aware of the subject of discussion before they arrived for the session. The research was carried out in July 1982, two months after the end of the first series of Q.E.D.

---

(4)   Three programmes were chosen to represent different styles of presentation. They were: 'Music, Music, Music', 'Spy in the Sky' and 'Proof of the Pudding'.

Results

By and large, the issues that the producers had identified as central were also important to viewers, though whether this shows the extent of producers' understanding of their audience or the operation of some sort of self-fulfilling prophecy, is open to investigation. On a more detailed level, the research showed that the style of presentation, in terms of structure and content, was important in determining the extent to which viewers understood the programme and felt satisfied with it.

How did Q.E.D. fit in with other T.V. programmes?

As the executive producer had felt, it was clear that the idea of the Q.E.D. series was one which was warmly welcomed by viewers. They were enthusiastic about programmes from which they would learn something but which would not be didactic or dull. There seemed to be a gap between certain science/documentary programmes like Horizon and T.V. Eye, which covered interesting subjects and were rewarding to watch - but mentally exhausting; and others, like Tomorrow's World, which although they were not too demanding to watch could only touch on topics and not give any detailed information.

Q.E.D., therefore, could potentially fit about halfway along the continuum of science/documentary programmes, midway between the detailed, demanding programmes at one extreme, and the more superficial, easier programmes at the other extreme.

When viewers of the groups categorised the Q.E.D. programmes they had seen, they did in fact, place Q.E.D. in the middle of this spectrum. Initially, each of the programmes in the series was classified separately and they were seen as similar to cookery, nature, current affairs or humorous programmes. Gradually, however, a common category was abstracted: all the programmes were seen as informative. They were described as light, 'science for the layman', documentary programmes which were similar in general type to programmes like The World About Us, T.V. Eye, Tomorrow's World and, to a lesser extent, Horizon. However, this was a slightly uneasy classification because to some extent, Q.E.D. was seen as forming a new, different category of programmes. Since viewers tend to use existing categories to evaluate programmes, those which do not readily fit into any existing category are more difficult for viewers to accept.

Satisfaction with the programmes

Some programmes were received more favourably than others, but all programmes were felt to cover interesting subjects, in ways which were unusual and not at all didactic or 'heavy-handed'. However, certain criticisms emerged which were common to all the programmes covered in the research, and also seemed to be applicable to the other programmes in the series. This paper will concentrate on these common feelings since these were the ones which were of most use to the production team. It is important to stress, however, that the criticisms made by viewers were largely about peripheral aspects of the structure and presentation of the programme and, although important, did not in any way reflect a fundamental dislike of the programmes - rather, it ws because viewers had hoped for and expected such a lot from the Q.E.D. programmes, that they were left with a slight sense of disappointment when these hopes were not entirely fulfilled.

First of all, because they saw it as an informative series, viewers expected to learn from it. They felt that it would both inform and explain, but did not expect it to be dull, didactic or baffling. Since they felt it was a "layman's" series, viewers also expected to be able to understand Q.E.D. fairly easily.

Finally, viewers hoped that Q.E.D. would be interesting and entertaining. These hopes and expectations that viewers had of Q.E.D. were similar to the producers' intentions and aims for the programme.

The three things, therefore, that viewers were looking for in Q.E.D. were the three Reithian functions of television: to understand, to learn and to be entertained. Viewers' overall satisfaction with the Q.E.D. programmes partly depended on the extent to which they felt that their hopes had been met.

Did viewers understand the programmes?

Largely, viewers did understand the programmes and were interested in the subjects presented. However, there were parts in some programmes which were difficult to follow - not really because of the complexity of the subject matter or the content of the programme, but because of the structure and the way topics were presented. A common criticism was that the programmes were "bitty", "jumbled" or that "they jumped about". There seemed to be no logical order or thread running through the programmes and consequently viewers seemed to get a bit lost. Viewers stressed the importance of understanding why sequences followed each other, which would make the programme much easier to follow. One programme in which viewers did perceive a logical flow was better understood than the others.

On occasion, viewers found the 'experts' who contributed to the programmes confusing and too technical - one of the programmes which had no 'talking heads' was felt to be easier to understand. Viewers found a layman's exposition of the subject easier to follow; although this has to be traded off against the reduced credibility of laymen compared with 'experts'. Finally, the lack of clear aims also made the programmes difficult to follow. Viewers were unsure what they were supposed to understand from the programme or what the point of the programme was. Furthermore, there seemed, in some programmes, to be such a proliferation of aims that it was difficult either to understand the basic explanation of the topic or to follow any one aspect of the subject.

The difficulty in understanding which viewers occasionally seemed to experience frustrated their expectation that the programmes would be easy and non-demanding. It was exacerbated by the fact that viewers were interested in the subject matter and clearly wanted to understand what was being presented. It is important to stress, however, that the level of complexity of the content of the programme was by and large readily acceptable to viewers; their confusion seemed to be caused more by the structure and presentation of the programme.

Did viewers learn from the programmes?

Although for the most part viewers understood the programmes, they were not left with a sense that they had learnt much from them. This was partly due to a feeling that there was little information actually given in the programmes. There was a strong impression, common across the three programmes which were discussed in detail, that they were "padded" "shallow" "frothy" and with little substance and few hard facts. Again, this was exacerbated by viewers' hopes that they would gain quite a lot of solid information. There was a criticism that potentially interesting subjects had not been covered in any detail. Viewers did not equate simplicity of exposition with lack of content and clearly wanted a programme packed with information which was presented in simple terms. Additionally, viewers felt that the programmes were inconclusive, that there was no 'pay-off' at the end of the programme. Even if this would not increase the actual amount of information imparted, it seemed to provide a sense that something had been communicated, or proved, which viewers seemed to expect and want; and which was reinforced (for the few who had understood it) by the meaning of the series title: Q.E.D.

Did viewers find the programmes entertaining?

The third expectation which viewers had of the Q.E.D. programmes was that they would be entertaining. Most viewers found the programmes interesting and entertaining since many used a lighthearted, humorous approach which seemed to be enjoyed. However, some of the programmes were felt to be boring and repetitive. This was, in part, a defensive reaction because, contrary to their expectations, they did not find the programmes informative or easy to follow. The "old-fashioned" style of one of the programmes and the very slow pace of another of the programmes contributed to some viewers' lack of enjoyment. Enjoyment of the programmes was greatly increased when viewers understood and felt they learnt something from the programmes.

Reactions to different styles of presentation

The style of presentation seemed to be less important than the structure of the programme, since viewers' expectations seemed to be frustrated by a perceived lack of a coherent structure. However, it seemed that if viewers were able to understand and learn from a programme, variations in style and novel approaches were tolerated - even welcomed. The programme which had the most traditional format came closest to meeting viewers' expectations, but viewers were by no means wedded to a traditional 'documentary style' approach and enjoyed the more innovative 'off-beat' styles of some of the programmes.

Did viewers see the Q.E.D. programmes as a series?

The short answer to that question was no. Each programme in the series had its own title which was featured in the opening sequence. Although this was preceded in all cases with the Q.E.D. logo, the logo was easily missed and in most cases viewers did not link the programme title with Q.E.D. even when they were aware of the series title. Also the programme listings in the daily newspapers did not always include 'Q.E.D.'. All of these factors accounted for the low recognition of the series title 'Q.E.D.'

However, the low profile of Q.E.D. was not the only reason that viewers did not perceive the programmes as a series. Even viewers who had seen all the programmes in the series did not notice a common link which would identify them as part of the same series. The programmes were different from each other in terms of style of presentation, subject matter, level of complexity and the perceived quality of the programmes. Wide diversity in <u>all</u> these variables meant that a series identity was not built up, although diversity in <u>some</u> variables (which was one of the aims of the series) was compatible with building a series identity. It seemed important to viewers that what they saw as the 'quality' of the programmes and the level of complexity should be the same for all programmes; however the subject matter and, to a lesser extent, the style of presentation could be much more diverse.

Viewers felt that the series' identity could also be built up by more obvious use of the series' title, trails for the next programme at the end of each programme and by having a common presenter 'fronting' all the programmes. There were difficulties, however, associated with having a common presenter since viewers felt that it was important that the presenter should be knowledgeable and credible, but that this would be difficult to achieve over a wide range of subjects. A further disadvantage of using a common presenter is it would reduce the element of diversity and 'surprise' which Q.E.D. aims for. Over time, it seems probable that a series identity could be built up with more prominent use of the series title and slightly greater homogeneity in terms of the quality and level of complexity, between the programmes.

The Response From The Media Practitioners

It was on Monday 13th December 1982 that the Q.E.D. troops assembled to hear the results of Anne Laking's project. Apart from myself, most of the team had been sceptical of the project but during the morning the attitude changed quite clearly as more and more usable and helpful information was revealed.

Firstly, of course, it was very satisfactory to know that the viewers felt the basic idea for the series was welcome and that the subjects were interesting. That was the major worry removed; we were at least on the right road. But I was also worried that we included much variation in style - a variety that I wanted to maintain. No, it seemed that was OK. We could continue to experiment stylistically.

It was good to know that the level of content seemed right. Clearly we would stick with it and neither move up or down market, but equally clearly we had to sort out our structure, our storytelling. The viewers needed to know more clearly where they were going. In our programmes since then we have done this. For example, "Bugging in Six Easy Lessons" was literally divided into six parts each with a sub-title. And "Why things go wrong" had a clear statement at its start on the aims and structure of the programme. And I have selected more subjects with a clear narrative structure - "Faster than the Sun" was set inside a single flight of Concorde; "Simon's War" was the chronological story of a Falklands war casualty; "Big Day at Black Rock" was 24 hours in an attempt on the land speed record.

Since then I have shied away from indeterminate subjects which could have no clear ending, no "conclusion". It's interesting that "Bend, Bend, Bend", a film - now shown twice - that sat on the fence over paranormal metal bending, has had AI's of 69 and 73 against series averages of 83 and 81. And on a parallel issue we have tried to keep the flow of new information going throughout the programmes - but without increasing its complexity. In viewing the rough cuts of our films, I am constantly looking for those nuggets of information that produce the response "Oh, I didn't know that" and can be used in conversation in the pub or at the bus stop next morning.

One other change I made was to relax my attitude towards talking heads. There were no indications that the audience reacted against them except when they were too complex, boring or just plain bad. Indeed I had a feeling that by discouraging talking heads I had depersonalised some programmes too much. However my main battle cry was still "show me; don't tell me".

Finally, and perhaps most importantly, I had to make the series seem more like a series - and yet maintain that variety. What I decided to do was essentially cosmetic: I would make the series seem more like a series but still keeping the variety of style, of presentation and of subject matter. First, we would find a regular series narrator with a readily identifiable voice: eventually we chose the delightful Irish tones of Dr. Anthony Clare. Second, I would litter the place with Q.E.D. logos: they now appear at both ends of the programmes whereas, for the first series, the logo was used only at the start. Thirdly, I would use the initials "Q.E.D." much more generally in publicity material, promotions and Radio Times billings. And often we have used it in narration. For example "..the Q.E.D. stuntman" appeared frequently in "Acts of God" and often we now use lines like "so Q.E.D. set up an experiment". Finally, I would build into the end of each programme a trail for the next one. We did this for series two but dropped it for series three for practical reasons.

And has it all worked? Well, it's now September 1983 and there have been three series of Q.E.D. on BBC-1.

And the audience data look like this:-

Table 5:

			Audience Millions	AI
Series	1	BBC-1	4.8	81
	2	BBC-1	6.1	81
	3	BBC-1	7.5	83

Still not an average of 8 million but getting very close! Nearly Q.E.D.

Special Reports issued during 1982

Radio (General)

In-Car Listening (LR/82/82): The nature and extent of radio listening in vehicles.

Preferences on Radio Between 10.30 p.m. and Midnight (SP/82/03): Preferences for late evening listening were studied using a large scale sample of adults.

Radio (Network)

Woman's Hour (LR/82/1): Opinions of the programme explored during group discussions.

2's Company (LR/82/39 and LR/82/174): The market for speech programme in the 2 to 5 a.m. slot was examined using a sample of night time listeners, and an analysis of the views of correspondents to the programme.

Radio 4 On Tour in the West Midlands (LR/82/53): Awareness of the week, the image of Radio 4 in the area, and the week's effect on audience size.

Radio 4 On Tour in the South-West (LR/82/85): Assessment of the effectiveness of the publicity for Radio 4's week in the South-West.

Action Special 1982 (LR/82/149): Awareness and impact of a BBC/Manpower Services Commission campaign to help young people find alternatives to unemployment.

Proms '82 (SP/82/09): Research among prom-goers to assess their views of the 1982 Season and possible future changes.

The Financial World Tonight (SP/82/21): Listeners' reactions and an assessment of the total potential audience.

Radio (Local)

Radio Norfolk (LR/82/2): A study of attitudes towards, and opinions of the BBC's first restricted local radio station.

Radio Nottingham: The East Midlands Experiment in Sharing "Afternoon Special" (LR/82/84): Local support was discovered for sharing a popular afternoon programme on Radio Nottingham with three other East Midlands radio stations.

Radio Furness (LR/82/116): A pre-broadcast study for the BBC's first opt-out local radio station.

Listeners' Opinions of "Barbed Wireless" (SP/82/10): A small-scale study of a young people's programme for Radio Derby.

Radio and Television

Listening and Viewing in the Channel Islands (LR/82/83): Availability to listen to proposed new local radio stations, and preferences among the local population.

Elderly People's Use of the Media (SP/82/03): Preferences and needs among the elderly were studied.

Listening and Viewing Among Welsh Speaking People in Wales (LR/82/10):

Television

Potential Topics for Continuing Education Series (VR/82/8: VR/82/96 and SP/82/06): Interest in a series on each of the following was investigated: World Development; Crime and Punishment; Race Relations; The British Economy; Health and Farming Problems (VR/81/363).

"Afternoon Magazine Programme" (VR/82/137): Group discussions were held to find out what potential viewers would like a new afternoon programme to provide.

Newsnight: Viewing, Non-viewing and Opinions (VR/82/28): The audience for 'Newsnight', their opinions and the effects of programme timing.

Grapevine (VR/82/75): Group discussions about the Community Programme Unit's self-help series.

So You Want to Stop Smoking? (VR/82/95 and SP/82/04): The impact and effectiveness of the series was the subject of a large scale evaluation project.

Taking Stock: Background Research (VR/82/94): Data was gathered about the interests, needs, hopes, anxieties of people aged between 50 and 60.

Daytime Viewing and Preferences Among a Sample of Unemployed Respondents (VR/82/135): A small-scale study of the activities of the unemployed as background for a proposed daytime series.

The Opinions of Disabled Viewers of "Open Door" Attitudes (VR/82/140): Response of disabled viewers to a programme on the attitudes of the able-bodied towards the disabled.

Television News: Self-Estimates of Viewing (VR/82/142): Estimates of the proportion of the population who claimed to watch occasionally or regularly were compared in August 1981 and March 1982.

John Craven's Newsround: The Falklands Crisis (VR/82/143): A short poll among children and adults on facts related to the Falklands Crisis.

Viewers' Reactions to Q.E.D. (SP/82/01): Group discussions to study reactions to this new Science and Features series.

Nationwide (SP/82/11): The effect of changes of format on audience size and attitudes.

The Nine O'Clock News (SP/82/15): A comparison of attitudes to, and viewing of the 9 O'Clock News and News At Ten, to assess the impact of changes in the 9 O'Clock News presentation.

How People Find Out About Programmes (SP/82/16 and 17): The way viewers find out about programmes, especially the use of programme trails.

BBC's Computer Literacy Project - An Evaluation (SP/82/22): An evaluation of the television series, the micro-computer system and 'The Computer Book'.

New Technology

Showcable: Subscribers' Reactions (VR/82/7 and SP/82/14): Results of a two-year cable experiment by the BBC and Visionhire.

Effects of National Teletext Month (VR/82/55): The effects of a government-sponsored publicity campaign on public awareness of teletext, examined in 2 national surveys.

Research for CEEFAX (1) (SP/82/08): Public reactions to teletext and the public's view of information that it should provide.